ᵗʰᵉ Irish

Lieutenant Governor Frank O'Bannon and his wife, Judy, show their Irish pride while marching in the 1989 St. Patrick's Day Parade in Indianapolis.

Volume 1
Peopling Indiana

the Irish

WILLIAM W. GIFFIN

INDIANA HISTORICAL SOCIETY PRESS
Indianapolis, 2006

Printed in Canada

This book is a publication of the
Indiana Historical Society Press
450 West Ohio Street
Indianapolis, Indiana 46202-3269 USA
www.indianahistory.org
Telephone orders 1-800-447-1830
Fax orders 317-234-0562
Online orders @ shop.indianahistory.org

Portions of this book previously appeared in *Peopling Indiana: The Ethnic Experience*, ed. by Robert M. Taylor Jr. and Connie A. McBirney (Indianapolis: Indiana Historical Society, 1996).

The paper in this publication meets the minimum requirements of American National Standard for Information Sciences—Permanence of Paper for Printed Library Materials, ANSI Z39.48-1984

Library of Congress Cataloging-in-Publication Data

Giffin, William Wayne, 1938–
 The Irish / William W. Giffin.
  p. cm.—(Peopling Indiana ; v.1)
 Includes bibliographical references and index.
 ISBN 0-87195-193-2 (alk. paper)
 1. Irish Americans—Indiana—History 2. Immigrants—Indiana—History. 3. Indiana—Emigration and immigration—History.
4. Ireland—Emigration and immigration—History.
I. Title. II. Series.
 F535.I6G54 2006
 977.200491'62–dc22
                                                    2005056808

Contents

Foreword

THOUGH INDIANA IS NOT KNOWN AS AN ETHNICALLY diverse state, its history and character have been indelibly shaped by the influx of people into the United States in the last two centuries. The book, *Peopling Indiana: The Ethnic Experience*, edited by Robert M. Taylor Jr. and Connie A. McBirney and published by the Indiana Historical Society in 1996, was the culmination of a multiyear ethnic history project of the Indiana Historical Society that brought together thirty original essays that surveyed the races and nationalities that at one time or another settled in the Hoosier state. Focusing on some fifty groups, the book's collection revealed what some may have considered a surprising range of diversity.

Essays in *Peopling Indiana* explore the histories of immigrants to Indiana from countries such as China, Great Britain, Greece, Palestine, Vietnam, Bulgaria, Switzerland, Sweden, Mexico, Canada, India, Germany, Japan, Korea, and the former Yugoslavia, and they also examine such groups as Native Americans, African Americans, and Jewish Americans. A thoughtful introduction by John Bodnar surveys the state's ethnic history, and an appendix by Gregory Rose provides data on Indiana's ethnic distribution in 1850. Other appendixes display tabular material on ethnic rankings at specific times, and charts throughout the book help the reader visualize the changing character of Indiana ethnicity.

By investigating kinship, social gatherings, occupations, education, recreation, and organizational membership, *Peopling Indiana* reveals the richness of immigrant life in the state and facilitates understanding of either the depth of a group's ethnic identity or the degree of its assimilation. The essays take the reader on historical journeys with all kinds of groups as they planted roots in Indiana, launched benevolent and social organizations, set up lodges and fraternities, built churches and synagogues, established political parties and labor unions, sponsored schools, worked in factory and field, enjoyed holidays, wept at weddings and funerals, and attempted to pass on a legacy of those things in their history and culture that characterized and distinguished them. In so doing, the book shows that individuals and families reached an accommodation, for better or worse, between their new home and the life they left behind. They managed to maintain what they could of their culture while adapting, some more eagerly than others, to the contingencies of a host state and country. Their stories of sacrifice, failure, and triumph are timeless.

The histories in *Peopling Indiana* remind us of the dynamic framework of retaining and adjusting that characterizes people moving and settling in any place. Now some of those histories, for the largest of Indiana's ethnic groups, will be presented in a series of books, edited and published by the Indiana Historical Society (IHS) Press. The series title, Peopling Indiana, reflects the series' association with the book; each volume will include an updated essay from the *Peopling* book, illuminating the migratory, settlement, and community-building experiences of the essay's subject group. The books in the series will be updated by the original author(s) whenever possible, and each will be fully illustrated and indexed.

The Irish is the first volume in this new series. *Peopling Indiana* author William W. Giffin has updated his original essay to include the activities of Irish Americans in Indiana through the end of the twentieth century. Through new information revealing a revival of

Irish traditions in Indiana and America and a collection of recent photographs, the first volume in the Peopling Indiana series celebrates the revival of Irish traditions at the beginning of the twenty-first century, from Celtic dancing and storytelling to ethnic cultural and service organizations such as the Ancient Order of Hibernians and Indiana's Emerald Society.

Although the *Peopling Indiana* book graciously thanks the many people who helped to research, write, compile, and edit it, staff members of the Family History Publications section of the IHS Press should be acknowledged for their assistance in editing this volume. Editorial assistant Amanda C. Jones proofread the new essay against the original and checked the facts and sources in the new material. Jones began the process of gathering illustrations for the book; and her successor, intern Bethany Natali, did an admirable job of pulling all the illustrations and permissions-to-publish together. Editorial assistant Geneil Breeze assisted Natali with the illustrations, making several useful and interesting recommendations. Breeze and editor, M. Teresa Baer, were responsible for copyediting the book, and Baer oversaw its production.

M. Teresa Baer
(with Robert M. Taylor Jr. on the *Peopling Indiana* book)

Introduction

THIS BRIEF HISTORY SURVEYS THE IRISH PRESENCE IN INDI-
ana from the early eighteenth century through
the twentieth century. It is meant to inform and
interest the general reader curious about ethnic
life in the United States and about Irish American
history in particular. The many photographs in this
book bring to life aspects of the Irish in Indiana's
past. Irish life in the Wabash and Erie Canal construction camps, the role of Indiana's Irish in the
1860s Fenian invasion of Canada, and the late twentieth century rebirth of Irish identity in Indiana are
examples of topics that add interest to this narrative. It is also hoped that this book will induce read-
ers of Irish ancestry to help advance understanding
of the Irish American experience by preserving the
documentary records and oral traditions of their
families, organizations, and institutions. This volume is also intended to serve as a starting point
for scholars interested in studying Irish themes in
Indiana and to encourage scholarly research and
writing on this neglected subject.

Published studies centered on the Irish in Indiana have been scarce. Elfrieda Lang's journal arti-
cle "Irishmen in Northern Indiana Before 1850"
appeared in 1954. Scholarly publications focusing
on the Irish in Indiana theme were not seen again
until the end of the century. A fine entry called
"Irish" was included in the 1994 publication of the
Encyclopedia of Indianapolis. An essay entitled "Irish"

was published in 1996 in *Peopling Indiana: The Ethnic Experience*, edited by Robert M. Taylor Jr. and Connie A. McBirney. A somewhat revised and updated version of the "Irish" essay in *Peopling Indiana* is presented in the following pages.[1] Information about various aspects of Irish life in Indiana are given in secondary sources concerning many topics of local, state, regional, and church history. These sources include unpublished theses and dissertations as well as books and journal articles. Primary sources used in this study to document the Irish experience in Indiana include published correspondence, newspapers, city directories, state and federal documents, and oral interviews.

Studies of the Irish in Indiana can elucidate the midwestern dimension of the Irish American experience. This is needed for a more complete Irish American history. Early histories of the Irish in the United States emphasize emigration from Ireland to the Northeast and to large cities in all regions because the Irish were most heavily distributed in these areas. Excepting Chicago, for example, these histories give relatively little notice to cities and states north and west of the Ohio River. The geographical focus has widened since 1960, especially in the past decade or so. An analysis of the Irish in Butte, Montana, is one instance of this. Recent monographs examine the Irish in the South as a region. Other new books cover the Irish in a single state in the Midwest. This Indiana survey joins recently published histories about the Irish statewide in Iowa, Minnesota, and Wisconsin.[2]

This book reveals distinctive aspects of Irish life in Indiana that were at variance from the Irish American experience elsewhere, notably in great urban centers and in northeastern states. It also shows that the Irish in Indiana had experiences generic to Irish Americans and ethnic groups everywhere in the country. This book provides a synthesis of secondary source material on the Irish in Indiana enriched by a measure of original research. It calls attention to traditional and current issues in the ongoing historiographical dialogue about Irish Americans. It comments on old themes such as immigration, acculturation, upward mobility, and politics while bringing attention to new ones, including gender, historical memory, return to Ireland, and transatlantic migration. It provides a selected bibliography for the general reader seeking additional current literature about the Irish. This volume concludes by calling scholars' attention to questions about the Irish in Indiana needing further research and writing and to the kinds of primary source materials that may yield some answers to them.

1. | Colonists and Settlers:
1740–1832

Descendants of the Emerald Isle entered Indiana in the eighteenth century. The Irish were represented among the relatively few fur traders and pioneers who were active in Indiana before it became a state in 1816. They also participated in the settlement of the new state through the 1820s. Irish immigrants came to the state of Indiana in great numbers for the first time during the years 1832 to 1860. The influx of Irish natives peaked in Indiana during the period 1860 to 1920, when the Irish were most identifiable as an ethnic group. The history of the Irish in Indiana from 1920 to 2000 is largely the story of descendants of immigrants from Ireland who came to the United States in the nineteenth century.

The Irish appeared on the Indiana record in the early eighteenth century when the occupants of the territory north of the Ohio River were the Miami, other Native Americans, and French colonial inhabitants. Immigrants from Ireland formed the largest non-English foreign-born contingent arriving in the English colonies in the eighteenth century. These Irish newcomers were largely people of Scottish ancestry whose families had settled in Northern Ireland (Ulster). Until the 1760s English colonists (including the Irish) made no attempt to settle west of Pennsylvania in territory occupied by native people and claimed by France. English colonial businessmen had little success breaking into

BY WILLIAM HENRY HARRISON,

GOVERNOR OF THE INDIANA TERRITORY, AND SUPERINTENDANT OF INDIAN AFFAIRS.

WHEREAS *Benoist Bezayou* of the county of *Knox* hath made application for permission to trade with the *Miami* nation of Indians, and hath given bond according to law, for the due obſervance of all the laws and regulations for the government of the trade with Indians that now are, or hereafter may be enacted and eſtabliſhed, licenſe is hereby granted to the ſaid *Benoist Bezayou* to trade with the ſaid *Miami* nation, at their town *on the Wabash* and thereto ſell, barter and exchange with the individuals of the ſaid nation, all manner of goods, wares and merchandizes, conformably to the laws and regulations aforeſaid; but under this expreſs condition and reſtriction, that the ſaid *Benoist Bezayou* ſhall not, by *his* ſervants, agents or factors, carry or cauſe to be carried to the hunting camps of the Indians of ſaid nation, any ſpecies of goods or merchandize whatſoever, and more eſpecially ſpirituous liquors of any kind ; nor ſhall barter or exchange the ſame, or any of them, in any quantity whatever, on pain of forfeiture of this licenſe, and of the goods, wares and merchandize, and of the ſpirituous liquors which may have been carried to the ſaid camps, contrary to the true intent and meaning hereof, and of having *his* bond put in ſuit: and the Indians of the ſaid nation are at full liberty to ſeize and confiſcate the ſaid liquors ſo carried, and the owner or owners ſhall have no claim for the ſame, either upon the ſaid nation, or any individual thereof, nor upon the United States.

This licenſe to continue in force for one year, unleſs ſooner revoked.

GIVEN under my hand and ſeal, the *Thirtieth* day of *December* , in the year of our Lord one thouſand eight hundred and *Seven*

Willm Henry Harrison

Indiana State Archives

A license to trade furs with the Miami Indians. Irish immigrants, along with the French, were among the earliest fur traders in Indiana.

the fur trade with the western Indians who dealt almost exclusively with the French. Catering to Indians by placing trading posts near their towns, France established Fort Ouiatenon, Fort Miamis, and Post Vincennes on the Wabash-Maumee water route. This virtual French monopoly of the western fur trade was broken by English colonists during the 1740s.[1]

A native of Ireland played a major role in this turn of events. George Croghan arrived in Pennsylvania after emigrating from Dublin in 1741. He shortly established an extensive fur trading enterprise in the Great Lakes region. His trade connections extended westward to the Wabash River. During the 1740s Croghan and his Pennsylvania associates obtained an increasing share of the western fur trade at the expense of the French. By the end of the decade some of the Miami and other natives of the Wabash country were traveling to Pickawillany (in present-day western Ohio) to deal with the Irishman. According to a frontier histo-rian, Croghan was successful in winning Native American customers because he was fair and tactful in his dealings with them, unlike fur traders of English descent who often showed their contempt for Indians. Also, the man from Dublin was successful because he was unusually enterprising and because he offered quality trade goods at low prices.[2] A Croghan biographer, describing him as a fascinating character with an unusu-

Ireland on a global map.

ally generous and charitable nature, wrote: "Croghan took snuff, drank heavily, loved to dress richly, and to live on a grand scale. When he addressed himself to his contemporaries, his native background stood out like a beacon—orally, in his strong, Irish brogue, and, on paper, in a handwriting and spelling so unschooled as to approach illiteracy. A master of conviviality, his easy good nature made him an idol on the frontier."[3]

Becoming aware of his amicable contacts with Native Americans, officials of colonial Pennsylvania and the British government engaged Croghan's services in Indian diplomacy. Croghan became the leading negotiator with the western Indian nations before the American Revolution. The aim of the diplomacy was to loosen the ties between France and the Miami and other western nations. Croghan was successful in promoting this goal before 1754. For example, while at Pickawillany in 1751 he received a group of Wea and Piankashaw from the Wabash country and accepted their petition to be taken under English protection. The rivalry between the fur traders of England and France caused friction between the two nations, which brought them into armed conflict. Croghan failed

MapArt, Cartesia Software, 1995; modified by Connie A. Rendfeld, Indiana Historical Society, 2006 to persuade most of the Native Americans not to side with France in the ensuing French and Indian War. However, the Irishman apparently did not lose his favorable reputation among the natives of the western country. He accomplished another assignment in Indian diplomacy after the war with France. Croghan was called upon to negotiate an end to Pontiac's War, which involved many Indian nations across the Great Lakes region. Native American forces captured most of the British forts in that area in 1763. Croghan's diplomatic expedition took him to Vincennes and to Fort Ouiatenon on the Wabash River (near present-day Lafayette) in 1765. Finally Croghan met with Pontiac, who was the Ottawa leader of the Indian campaign. Pontiac agreed to make peace on Croghan's promise that the British would not permit settlements in the western country. In large measure Pontiac's War had been a response to Native American concern about the consequences of an influx of colonial settlers into lands just beyond the Allegheny Mountains, which had begun for the first time at the opening of the decade.[4]

During the rest of the eighteenth century relatively few people migrated from the East to settle in Indiana or in the Great Lakes region, but some of those who did so were of Irish descent. Croghan's promise to Pontiac related to the Royal Proclamation of 1763, which prohibited unauthorized settlement west of the Allegheny Mountains. In the face of this proclamation, population movement beyond the Alleghenies was minimal, and there was no English colonial settlement in Indiana before the War for Independence. Settlers from the states began arriving in Indiana during the American Revolution. Settlement was confined to three areas of southern Indiana until the end of the century. The earliest and westernmost of the new settlements was along the Wabash River at Vincennes. A few of the migrants arrived in 1779 when the place was in the hands of an American army under the command of George Rogers Clark, but more of them located there after the end of the war. By 1786 the Vincennes area contained a few hundred English-

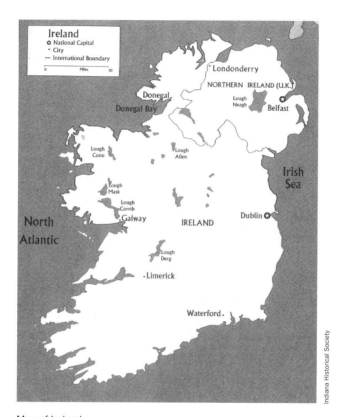

Map of Ireland.

speaking newcomers whose cultural heritages conflicted with those of the old French inhabitants of the town. The resulting ethnic friction led Colonel J. M. P. Le Gras, a local magistrate, to see many of the English-speaking newcomers as aggressive and undesirable. Le Gras found Daniel Sullivan to be especially troublesome. Undoubtedly Sullivan was of Irish origin. The early eastern settlements were on Clark's Grant near the Falls of the Ohio River (in present-day Clark and Harrison Counties) and in the Gore (near the present Ohio boundary and including modern Dearborn County). The settlers of these areas were mainly old-stock Americans, a great proportion of whom were of Irish ancestry. The Irish-stock settlers of this period were largely, but not exclusively, related to persons who had emigrated from Northern Ireland and who had settled earlier in the backcountry of the Carolinas and in Kentucky.[5]

With the turn of the century came important changes for the people of Indiana. In 1800 the United States Congress created the Indiana Territory with Vincennes as its capital. The population of the territory increased from about 2,500 in 1800 to about 64,000 in

Map by the Indiana Geological Survey; county names by Bethany Natali.

Early Irish immigrants settled in southern Indiana counties such as Dearborn and Floyd.

1815. Newcomers located in the old eighteenth-century settlement areas in Indiana as well as in new areas such as the Ohio River towns in the southeast (Lawrenceburg, Vevay, Madison, and Jeffersonville). The ethnic characteristics of the territorial population did not change much after 1800. Yet national diversity was somewhat greater, and the presence of the foreign-born was more evident during the Indiana territorial period. Some Irish natives living in Indiana were well-known to the territory's citizenry. William Prince was born in Ireland in 1772. After immigrating to the United States, Prince moved to Knox County, settling there by 1800. Prince married a woman of French descent, Therese Tremble, and took an active role in the public life of Vincennes. At various times during the territorial years he was Knox County sheriff, Vincennes postmaster, and county justice of the peace. Prince was known throughout Indiana as a member of the territorial council chosen in 1809 and as territorial auditor (1810–13).[6] James Dill was another highly visible native of Ireland. He located in Dearborn County after living in Kentucky. Dill was an avid supporter of territorial governor William Henry Harrison, who often appointed him to office. Dill made a vivid impression when serving in court as prosecuting attorney. One of his contemporaries wrote: "When Gen. Dill appeared in court, it was in the full costume of the gentleman of the last century—his knee breeches and silver buckles and venerable cue neatly plaited and flowing over his shoulders, seemed a mild protest against the leveling tendencies of the age; but nothing could impair the hold which the . . . courtly and witty Irishman had on the people of this county."[7]

Natives of Ireland were the first settlers in some areas of the Indiana Territory. James McGuire was born in 1785 at the seaport town of Dundalk in Ireland's Leinster province. McGuire joined the English army when an adolescent. He traveled with his regiment to Canada and subsequently made his way to Ohio. In 1808 McGuire moved to Lawrenceburg, Dearborn County, where he entered the

Indiana territorial militia and rose through its ranks. McGuire removed from Lawrenceburg to the Dearborn County countryside and thereby became the first settler of Laughery Township. One of his neighbors wrote: "When I moved to Laughery, in 1814, Major James McGuire lived one mile below me in the block house kept up in time of war."[8] Likewise, John Kelso emigrated from Ireland to New York and from there moved to the Indiana Territory in 1813. The Irishman was the first settler in an area that became Kelso Township, Dearborn County.[9]

In 1813, when Kelso arrived in Dearborn County, the territorial capital was removed from Vincennes to Corydon, where steps were taken to advance the Indiana Territory toward statehood. The United States Congress authorized a state constitutional convention after the census of 1815 determined that the territory exceeded the congressionally mandated population requirement for statehood. The Irish participated in the state-making process in Indiana. The constitutional convention held at Corydon in 1816 was composed of forty-three elected delegates, who apparently represented an approximate cross section of the territory's population with respect to nativity. Eleven of the delegates were natives of northern states, and twenty-six were natives of southern states. Six of the delegates had been born in European countries, four in Ireland, one in Germany, and one in Switzerland. Convention delegates Patrick Beard, James Dill, William Graham, and David Robb were natives of Ireland. When Indiana became the nineteenth state in the Union in 1816, its Irish population was still largely composed of descendants of immigrants from Northern Ireland. As most other pioneers, the Irish lived in the southern third of Indiana where most of them were involved in homestead farming.[10]

The 1815 population census of the Indiana Territory was taken in a seminal year in history. The Atlantic world entered an era of peace following the end of the War of 1812 in America and the conclusion of the Napoleonic Wars in Europe. These armed conflicts had almost completely stopped immigration to the United States during the previous two decades. The peace permitted the resumption of emigration from Europe. During the next one hundred years immigration to the United States occurred on a massive scale. The initial period of this new mass immigration was 1815–60. The total number of immigrants arriving in America increased dramatically each passing decade with the result that a grand total of about five million immigrants entered the United States during the period. The newcomers came mainly from the countries of northern and western Europe. Especially large numbers of immigrants came from the British Isles and from the German provinces. Ireland led all countries by sending about two million people to the United States. The Irish immigrants came from all the provinces of Ireland, but compared to the past, relatively few of them originated in Ulster. Many factors combined to bring about this mass immigration. Some rural people had been displaced by forces of industrialization and modern scientific farming that were on the rise in northern and western Europe in the first half of the nineteenth century. The catastrophic potato famine in Ireland during the 1840s was a factor contributing to the extraordinary scale of emigration from Erin. In addition, immigrants had countless individual motives for pulling up roots. As did most European immigrants of the period, the bulk of the Irish newcomers located in the northeastern quadrant of the United States between 1815 and 1860. Indiana was not among the states that received the greatest numbers of Irish immigrants during this period. Indeed, fewer foreign-born persons located in Indiana than in many northeastern states.[11]

Yet an unprecedented increase in the number of Irish immigrants in Indiana occurred during the years from 1816 through 1860. Meanwhile, Indiana passed through its pioneer phase when homestead farms were isolated by the absence of transportation improvements. In the three decades before the Civil War the construction of roads, canals, and railroads reduced the isolation of country folk, and commercial farming expanded. Further, the pace of industrialization and urbanization increased.

There was a small increase in Irish immigration to Indiana during the years 1816–32. Irish Catholic newcomers also became somewhat more visible in the population during this period. Although no systematic statistical record of the foreign-born was made, the presence of Irish natives was recorded in comments made by contemporaries. Some of the commentators were early travelers whose observations were later published. Isaac Reed, a Presbyterian missionary, noted that when he resided in New Albany in 1818 some of the town's inhabitants were from Ireland.[12] Karl Postel, a foreign traveler touring Indiana during the 1820s, also referred to the Irish. He wrote: "For adventurers of all descriptions, Indiana holds out allurements of every kind. Numbers of Germans, French, and Irish, are scattered in the towns, and over the country, carrying on the business of bakers, grocers, store, grog shops, and tavern keepers."[13]

The history of the Catholic Church in Indiana provides the best source of information about the Irish during 1816–32. The clergy and parishioners of the Catholic Church in this state were still predominantly French. French Jesuit priests had introduced the Wabash country to Catholicism, and Vincennes had become a center for the church's activities during the French colonial era. Missionary priests had been attending to the spiritual needs of Catholics outside of Vincennes since the early eighteenth century. By 1830 Catholic families lived in Vincennes, Princeton, Washington, Evansville, New Albany, St. Mary-of-the-Knobs, Vevay, Dover, Montgomery, Mount Pleasant, Columbus, Shelbyville, Indianapolis, Fort Wayne, and South Bend. The Catholic Church estimated that there were 20,000 Indiana Catholics in a total state population of about 345,000 in 1830. The Catholic population was composed chiefly of persons of French and English stock. The latter were related to English Catholic families that had immigrated to

Maryland and then migrated to Kentucky before coming to Indiana. Yet the Catholic record of the time contained evidence that Irish people were among the communicants of the church in Indiana. For example, Irish immigrants settled in Dearborn County during the early years of statehood. In 1820 Catholic parishioners, who were mainly Irish and English, erected a log church building at Dover in Kelso Township. The parish was served by priests from Bardstown, Kentucky, who traveled a Bardstown, Cincinnati, and Vincennes circuit. Bishop Benedict Joseph Flaget of the Bardstown diocese was responsible for Catholics in Indiana during this period.[14]

Similarly, the Irish presence was recorded in the history of the Catholic Church in Floyd County. Irish immigrants were among the earliest settlers in the vicinity of Little Indian Creek in Lafayette Township. Nineteenth-century Floyd County historians referred to this area as the Catholic or Foreign Settlement. The Irish immigrants who located there included Thomas Pierce, who departed Ireland in 1818 and who lived for a time in Pennsylvania. In 1820 Pierce settled on Little Indian Creek, where he was a farmer and surveyor. He was apparently accompanied on his journey from Ireland by the Byrns family (county Louth), which was composed of a mother, five sons, and three daughters. Shortly after the arrival of Pierce and the Byrns family, the Catholic Church was organized on Little Indian Creek by Father Abraham, a Catholic priest from Bardstown, Kentucky. Pierce donated land for the church building. The Irish Catholic settlers erected a log church by the creek at the foot of the knobs. Other Irish newcomers joined the congregation after 1820. Nicholas Duffey and his large family located in the Catholic Settlement in 1821. John Coleman, also from Ireland, joined this Catholic community in 1825. He was one of the initial schoolteachers and early justices of the peace in that part of Floyd County. As the years passed, still other Irish immigrants came to this vicinity making it an even more identifiable Catholic settlement.[15]

In summary, the history of the Irish in Indiana between 1816 and 1832 resembled the Irish story earlier in the century. The number of Irish increased moderately, and they were generally found in the southern half of the state, especially in Ohio River counties. General settlement in northern Indiana was minimal in 1830. According to a distinguished state demographic historian, only twelve Irish people settled in northern Indiana between 1820 and 1830.[16] Pioneer farming continued to be the chief pursuit of the Irish. Irish Catholics in the population were somewhat more evident than in the past.

2. | Newcomers in an Age of Mass Immigration: *1832–1860*

THE IRISH POPULATION INCREASE IN INDIANA DURING THE period 1832–46 was substantially greater than it ever had been in the past. Significant numbers of Irish immigrants came to Indiana to work in canal construction during the 1830s. The Wabash and Erie Canal was Indiana's first major artificial waterway. The canal scheme was grandiose. It projected the linking of Lake Erie at Toledo with the Ohio River at Evansville. The canal was expected to connect Fort Wayne, Logansport, and Lafayette in the north to Terre Haute, Washington, and Evansville in the south. Canal construction was confined to the northernmost section during the first half of the decade. The influx of Irish construction workers began in 1832, marking the start of canal excavation at Fort Wayne. The canal project created a demand for construction workers that was too great to be met by the laborers available in northern Indiana. Labor procurers advertised in newspapers throughout the state. In August 1832 the *Indianapolis Indiana Journal* published an advertisement that stated: "'Cash for Canal Hands' We wish to employ laborers on the Wabash and Erie Canal, 12 miles west of Fort Wayne. The situation is healthy and dry. We will pay $10 per month for sober and industrious men."[1]

When such efforts to secure men in Indiana proved insufficient to meet canal needs, labor contractors acting in the interests of the canal traveled

Irish immigrants comprised much of the workforce of the proposed canal through Indiana.

through Ohio, Pennsylvania, and New York, attempting to recruit immigrants, most of whom were Irish and German. The canal agents offered a contract under which the immigrant would receive an advance on the cost of transportation to Indiana in exchange for a deduction from his wages. Most of the immigrants who accepted the terms stipulated by the Wabash and Erie Canal labor agents were Irish.[2]

There was little about Indiana canal construction work to recommend it to Irish immigrants in the East. Employment in canal excavation was hard and dirty, while in midsummer it was also hot and thirsty work. Canal diggers lived in primitive and unsanitary shelters, worked in unhealthy environments, and moved in social circumstances conducive to rowdiness and heavy drinking. Furthermore, workers were usually out of contact with the church of their faith. In addition to facing these repellant features of work and life on the canal, married Irish immigrants had to choose between two undesirable alternatives when deciding to take canal construction work in Indiana. A married man could choose to move west alone, thereby exposing himself and his family to problems of separation, or he could take his family with him to Indiana, thereby subjecting the family to the crudities inherent in life on a canal under construction.[3]

Another problem confronted the Irish immigrant considering an offer of canal work in Indiana. Many self-described canal agents were confidence men who bilked or exploited immigrants. An example reported in the *Fort Wayne Sentinel* (August 27, 1842) stated:

> A number of stone cutters, chiefly Irish, and many with their families, have arrived here the past week, from New York on their way to Lafayette to work on the canal. . . . They were engaged by G. M. Nash . . . who advertised in the New York papers and by bills posted . . . that he was authorized by Messrs. Moorehead & Co. of Lafayette to engage them to work on the canal. Nash got $6.50 from each and gave them passage to Toledo. From Toledo, Moorehead & Co. would give them passage to Lafayette, where their fares would be returned. The Company denies all knowledge of Nash and needs no stone-cutters since the locks are made of wood. These families are to be pitied. Induced by high wages, now [they have] . . . no money and no jobs.[4]

Eventually the Irish American press attempted to dissuade Irish immigrants from taking jobs in canal construction. Their aim was to shield natives of Ireland from fraud and exploitation. Nevertheless, many Irishmen continued to ignore this advice and went west as construction workers.

Irish newcomers worked in canal construction because it offered them comparatively high wages. The canal worker's wage was ten dollars a month in 1832. The monthly wage rose to thirteen dollars in 1837 as the demand for construction labor increased. These wages were high in comparison to the remuneration commonly available to Irish immigrants in eastern cities, where most Irishmen were required to work as unskilled laborers receiving the lowest wages. A large majority of the Irish came out of rural and agricultural backgrounds and consequently lacked manufacturing skills. Also, countless eastern employers refused to hire Irish Catholics except as unskilled laborers. Many Irish immigrants found canal employment alluring because it appeared to represent a way to escape from urban poverty in the East.[5]

The incursion of Irish canal workers into Indiana during the 1830s was undoubtedly substantial. It may be assumed that thousands of immigrants were hired for canal construction during the course of the decade. The total number is unknown because the state did not keep careful records concerning canal building, and it did not systematically count the immigrants working on the Wabash and Erie Canal in the 1830s. Yet sometimes the number of canal workers was officially reported. The *Journal of the House of Representatives of the State of Indiana* stated that 205 immigrants were hired for canal work from March to June 1833. Private observers noted that there were approximately 1,000 construction workers on the canal near Fort Wayne in the summer of 1833. There were from 1,000 to 2,000 immigrants working on the canal between Fort Wayne and Huntington in 1834 and in 1835. Indiana residents who witnessed the influx of immigrants were impressed by the scene. A Presbyterian minister in Fort Wayne, making a missionary report in 1834, wrote that great numbers of German and Irish immigrants were arriving there. The number of immigrants appeared to be great in comparison to the small size of villages in northern Indiana. The Fort Wayne population was less than nine hundred in 1830.[6]

Labor was arduous for the Irishmen excavating the Wabash and Erie Canal. The work required walking miles through the unpopulated countryside, wading through marshes, and removing trees in wooded areas. The chief activity was digging and shoveling dirt in the ditch, often under a blazing sun. The canal diggers worked under the supervision of canal contractors who organized them into labor gangs. In describing the work method, canal historian Paul Fatout wrote: "They built canal banks by using one-horse carts, usually four carts to a squad. Four men filled a cart, which then pulled away to dump the load on the fill perhaps a hundred yards distant. Shovelers, spacing the process so that they had a cart filled by the time an empty one returned, were on a sort of production belt that meant steady digging and heaving."[7]

An 1860 memoir recalling Fort Wayne in the early canal days described a view of the men working there. The memoir stated, "The 'Old Fort,' or rather one building of it, [was] tenanted by some Irish family. . . . The canal was being dug at that point, and eastward, and when the season for labor began, hundreds of Irishmen, and horses and carts, could be seen at one view."[8]

Life in a Wabash and Erie Canal labor camp was harsh. Irish immigrants were sheltered in crudely erected log shanties. A shantytown stretched over a great distance by the side of the excavation in each of the areas where the canal was under construction. The canal labor camp was a predominantly male society. Most Irish workers were single men or married men separated from their families. Father Stephen Badin, a Catholic priest, visited the canal west of Fort Wayne in 1834. In reference to the Irish in labor camps there, he wrote that there were "very few of the devout sex, and few children among them."[9] However, some canal workers were accompanied by their families. Father Simon Lalumiere, a Catholic priest serving in Terre Haute, recorded that he attended many families and single men when he visited Catholics on the Wabash and Erie Canal between Lafayette and Coal Creek in 1842.[10]

Some of the working and living conditions on the Wabash and Erie Canal were detrimental to the health of the men, women, and children in the labor camps. Mosquitoes were prevalent all along the canal route, and there were mosquito infestations in marshes and lowlands on the canal line. Consequently, those working or living at the canal excavation commonly came down with the ague and other malarial fevers spread by disease-bearing insects. Illness was also the consequence of conditions in the construction camps. The workers' shanties were inevitably unsanitary. The crude shelters were small, overcrowded, located in primitive settings, and occupied by men doing dirty labor. Further, apparently inadequate attention was given to the removal of waste from the camps. Illness naturally occurred in these circumstances. The Irish in the shantytowns suffered from dysentery and sometimes contracted cholera. Dysentery and the ague were physical trials but were rarely fatal. Other malarial fevers were more likely to cause death. Victims of cholera usually died. The high mortality rate for the Irish on the canal became legendary. The name of Richard Doyle, an Irish canal worker, was the first entry in the burial record started by Father Badin when he was a missionary priest at Fort Wayne. The link between mortality and canal building was symbolized by burial markers along the canal route near Fort Wayne.[11]

Irish newcomers constructing canals in Indiana experienced other indignities. In some respects they were treated as a class apart from others. They carried the stigma of being poor people in an affluent land. Father Badin characterized the canal workers from Ireland as "the lower class of the Irish."[12] Canal contractors regarded Irishmen as unqualified to be employed as skilled laborers. Thus, men of other national backgrounds were engaged as skilled artisans and were paid higher wages to erect canal structures such as aqueducts. Meanwhile, Irishmen were hired to work with picks and shovels.[13] They were also set apart by their faith. The Irish Catholics were working in a heavily Protestant state, containing denominations and sects that were suspicious and fearful of the Catholic Church.[14]

The hard life in the Wabash and Erie Canal camps led many Irishmen to behave in ways inconsistent with accepted behavior in polite society in the 1830s. Excessive drinking and rowdiness were by-products of the canal construction experience.[15] Initially the canal commissioners attempted to preclude liquor problems. In 1832 canal contracts stated that, "the party of the first part [William Rockhill, contractor] shall not permit any workmen in his employ while they are engaged in constructing this Section [at Fort Wayne] to drink distilled spirits of any kind under the liability of forfeiting this contract at the option of the party of the Second part [Samuel Lewis, Canal Commissioner]."[16]

The liquor provisions of the canal contracts were enforced only for a short time. Drinking distilled spirits was common in Indiana pioneer society during the 1830s, and prohibition was not the prevailing viewpoint on liquor usage then. Subsequently, whiskey drinking was virtually sanctioned by canal contractors. In reference to the prevalence of drinking on the canal, one source stated, "and every gang of workmen boasted a 'jigger boss' whose duty it was to carry a large pail of whiskey along the line and issue a small drink or jigger when ever it seemed needed. His judgment was the only limit or guide."[17] Also shanties from which jiggers of whiskey were dispensed were set up along the canal works by local liquor merchants who took much of the workmen's wages. In 1834 Father Badin observed that the Irish canal laborers in Indiana were "too fond of drinking."[18] In the next decade Father Lalumiere reported, "I have much trouble with my Irish boys on the [Wabash and Erie] canal, they will drink."[19] The Irishmen drank because the liquor was available, because it was their custom, and because whiskey was seen as a medicinal for malaria. Undoubtedly the Irishmen who drank to excess saw whiskey as a means of diversion from loneliness and boredom and viewed the hard spirits as a way of temporary release from the grim work camp experience.[20]

Irish life on the Wabash and Erie Canal in the 1830s was further complicated by ethnic friction among the emigrants from Ireland. Two feuding groups of Irish canal workers were commonly known as the Fardowns and the Corkonians, whose animosities were rooted in the history of Ireland. The Fardowns were Protestants of Scottish ancestry who had emigrated from Ulster in Northern Ireland. The Corkonians were Catholic emigrants from Ireland. Corkonians and Fardowns were members of organized groups headed by leaders who advocated forms of ethnic nationalism. Some Irishmen entered these associations upon their arrival in the United States, for example, in New York City. Others joined later in canal construction areas. Undoubtedly, few Irish canal workers were active in these associations. However, at times most of the Irish on a canal were caught up in the feuds of the organized ethnic nationalists. The two groups shared a history of violent conflict in America as well as in Ireland. Men in the Corkonian and Fardown associations fought on canal construction projects in New York, Pennsylvania, and Maryland. Riots involving hundreds of men occurred on the Chesapeake and Ohio Canal, where the militia was called out after deaths and many injuries. This was the background of the conflict among Irish immigrants on the Wabash and Erie Canal.[21]

The troubles in Indiana began after September 1834 when Corkonian and Fardown members and leaders appeared on the Wabash and Erie Canal. These activists included men who had been involved in canal riots in the East. According to a contemporary source, during the following nine months Corkonians and Fardowns "manifested their ill will to each other by merciless beatings on such of each party as chanced to fall in the power of the other."[22] The Corkonians and the Fardowns occupied ethnically segregated construction camps—the Corkonians on the upper section of the canal line, and the Fardowns on the lower section of the line. Corkonians and Fardowns deliberately hired themselves to canal contractors on different parts of the line because they feared for their safety in ethnically mixed camps. The beatings were confined almost exclusively to the Irish laborers on the canal. Because local people were not involved, civil authorities made little effort to suppress the violence. In any case, law enforcement would have been difficult because there was no justice of the peace along great lengths of the canal in newly organized counties.

Hostilities escalated in the summer of 1835. Members of each party took great precautions for their safety before traveling from one part of the canal line to another. Tensions reached a critical level during the week before the July 12 anniversary of the Battle of the Boyne. The battle near Belfast in 1690 was an historic clash between Catholics and Protestants. The forces of King William of Orange, a Protestant, had defeated an Irish-French army supporting James II, a Catholic. Alarming stories circulated among the Irish in the canal camps as the anniversary approached. Corkonians and Fardowns heard essentially the same rumors— that their enemies would shortly attack their camp at night in an attempt to burn their shanties and murder them in their beds. Corkonian and Fardown camps were evacuated at night. Men, women, and children concealed themselves in the dark woods and avoided the use of light or fire so that their hiding places would not be revealed. In the daytime armed men worked on the canal. The work continued "until some idle report would get in circulation, that the other party was *marching* to fight them, at which times they would leave their work and hasten with great rapidity to the supposed point of danger."[23] Such alarms and responses were frequent during July 4–10.

Meanwhile, the two sides agreed to hold a showdown on the Boyne anniversary, and they chose a field for battle. On July 10 one of the canal engineers reported "that all the workmen on the lower end of the line were armed and marching to the reputed battlefield."[24] Indeed, both groups stopped working on July 10 and began to "march towards the centre of the line for a general battle."[25] According to the *Fort Wayne Sentinel*, eight hundred Corkonians, most of whom were armed, assembled at Lagro on July 10, while "at the same time about 250 armed Fardowns advanced to Wabash, seven miles from Lagro, on their way to attack their adversaries."[26] David Burr, a canal commissioner, reported that there were seven or eight hundred armed men with three or four hundred on a side. Burr met Fardown leaders as they moved up the canal line to a point near his residence, and then he talked to Corkonian spokesmen. Each side told Burr virtually the same story. The terror of possible violence at night could be borne no longer. Civil authority would not or could not protect them. They wished to work in peace, but they chose to fight in daytime to preclude nighttime depredations. A battle would end the problem by driving one of the parties away from the canal.[27]

Burr and some other local residents persuaded the two parties to suspend hostile activities while Burr attempted to negotiate a settlement. Father Lalumiere met with the Irish Catholics. According to a church historian, "His presence . . . made the laborers instantly disperse. He exhorted them to behave as true Irishmen, and true Catholics, worthy of the country of their adoption."[28]

Meanwhile, militia units and civil authorities from communities along the canal were called into action and made a show of force. Eight ringleaders were arrested and taken under a strong guard to Indianapolis because there was no secure jail in the area. Further, the authorities regarded the ringleaders as "the cause of contention" and therefore wished to separate them from their countrymen.[29] The jailed men were shortly freed by a writ of habeas corpus issued because of irregularities in the legal proceedings.[30] This event was summarized in Gov. Noah Noble's annual message to the legislature, in which he wrote, "During the past summer the foreign laborers upon the line of the canal, resuscitated some of their old party animosities, which so often were the cause of collision in their native country, Ireland, and while under great excitement, from five to seven hundred on a side assembled for several days, armed for battle, to the great terror of the citizens of that vicinity."[31] The anticipated battle among Irishmen was averted by the combination of diplomacy and force. Subsequently the canal board required each contractor to dismiss and blacklist any laborer who engaged in a brawl. Thereafter times were more peaceful. Yet the troubles among Irishmen did not end. *The Indianapolis Documentary Journal* reported fighting between Corkonians and Fardowns on the Central Canal in 1837. Meanwhile Bishop Simon Bruté of the Diocese of Vincennes urged the Catholic Church to devise means of deterring Irish immigrants from joining militant associations when they arrived in New York, to discover the leaders of such associations, and to find ways of appealing to the consciences of the men involved in them. Later these associations were condemned in a Catholic Church pastoral issued in New York.[32]

The Wabash and Erie Canal was not the only internal improvement project that attracted Irish construction workers to Indiana during the 1830s. An unknown number of Irishmen participated in early road building. National Road construction began at Richmond at the opening of the decade, continued to Indianapolis by the middle of the decade, and reached Terre Haute by 1839. National Road laborers receiving eight to twelve dollars a month were among the first Irish who settled in Indianapolis. Irish and German laborers working on the National Road augmented the Catholic population of Terre Haute. A construction boom in Indiana during the second half of the decade began in 1836 when the state legislature enacted the Mammoth Internal Improvements Act, which authorized eight construction projects

A portion of the canal in Indianapolis near Ohio and 13th streets, 1927.

Indiana Historical Society, P 0130

involving road, canal, and railroad building. The authorization provided for the construction of the Wabash and Erie Canal from Lafayette to the Ohio River, the Whitewater Canal in the state's southeast,
and the Central Canal through Indianapolis to northern and southern termini on the Wabash and Erie Canal. The implementation of
this grand scheme brought an even greater demand for construction
workers and higher wages paid to canal laborers. Thus, more Irish
immigrants came to Indiana to work on canals. For example, Irishmen were laboring on the Central Canal near Indianapolis by 1837.
However, all of the state-sponsored improvements projects were
stopped in 1839 when financing of the transportation scheme broke
down in the midst of the national economic depression that followed
the panic of 1837. The construction projects languished through the
first half of the next decade as the depression continued and as the
state was unsuccessful in reordering its finances. The demand for
canal diggers was minimal, and Irish immigrants had little incentive

to come to Indiana seeking canal and road construction work during that time.[33]

Irish Catholics who came to Indiana during 1832–46 were devoted to their faith. Immigrants separated from their families and friends in Ireland needed their church for support as they became accustomed to living in America, as well as for its spiritual guidance. Thus, the records of the Catholic Church reveal a notable part of

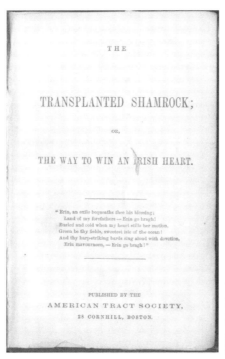

The title page from a Catholic Sunday School book, dated 1860. The Catholic Church played a big part in the lives of many Irish immigrants.

Irish history in Indiana. The Catholic Church in Indiana was initially hard-pressed in caring for the increasing number of Irish and German Catholic immigrants entering the state. Only four Catholic priests were serving in Indiana in 1834. Bishop Simon Bruté of the Diocese of Vincennes, formed in 1834, was responsible for the spiritual needs of Catholics in the whole state. In 1835 Bishop Bruté estimated that there were six to seven hundred Catholics at Fort

Wayne and fifteen hundred to two thousand more on the canal route. Catholics also lived elsewhere in the state. Father Badin and Father Lalumiere made trips to visit Catholics in the towns and in the construction camps on the Wabash and Erie Canal. Father Lalumiere enrolled Irish and German canal workers in a temperance society that he founded.[34]

The growth of the Catholic Church in Indiana was evidently related to the transportation improvements made in the 1832–46 period. The Catholic population particularly increased in towns located on recently constructed canals and roads as well as in towns on the Ohio River. During the 1830s Irish Catholics in Indiana towns and settlements were usually cared for by priests of French birth. Later, the national origins of the priests became more diverse as the number of Catholic parishioners and priests increased. By the early 1840s the list of priests serving in Indiana included Irish and German names. When a church building was not available in a town, a visiting priest said Mass in a local Catholic home as had been the custom in earlier times. In consequence of Catholic population growth in the early 1830s, Catholic parishes were organized, and Catholic churches were built in many Indiana towns in the years after 1835. The Catholic congregations were ethnic mixtures, composed largely of Irish and German parishioners.

The Catholic Church became more vital in Fort Wayne, Logansport, Lafayette, and other Wabash and Erie Canal towns after 1832. Most Catholics in Fort Wayne were of French ancestry before 1832. Yet Fort Wayne Catholics were predominantly Irish and German shortly after the arrival of canal construction workers in 1832. In the early 1830s Catholics were organized by Father Badin, who spoke fluent English. Father Badin collected money for a church building in 1834, when many of the Irish and Germans began arriving in Fort Wayne. Father Lalumiere visited Fort Wayne while touring the eastern part of the diocese in late winter 1835, where he noted that 150 Catholic families were worshiping in a newly erected chapel, apparently a small and plain structure. Father M. Ruff (born in Metz, France) attended Fort Wayne Catholics in 1835. He spoke French, English, and German. The Catholic population increased sufficiently to permit the assignment of the first resident pastor to Fort Wayne in 1840. He was Father Louis Mueller, who was of German birth. Due to personality differences, Father Mueller was eventually opposed by his parishioners, mainly the Irish and French. Father Mueller was required to confine himself to work among Catholics outside the city, chiefly Germans. The next resident priest was Father Julian Benoit, who arrived in 1840 and completed the building of St. Augustine Church, begun by his predecessor. During the 1840s Father Benoit apparently cared for the Irish and French communicants, while the German-speaking parishioners were attended by a priest of German birth who assisted Father Benoit.[35]

The arrival of Irish immigrants contributed to the growth of the Catholic Church in canal towns west of Fort Wayne. In the mid-1830s several Irish families settled at Lagro, a wheat-shipping port on the canal. Catholics erected a frame church in Lagro in 1838. The arrival of Irish workers made Peru a permanent Catholic mission station by 1834. A Catholic church was founded in Peru in 1838. There was an influx of Catholics into Logansport during the mid-1830s when the canal was being constructed in Cass County. In 1838 Father John Claude Francois organized a Catholic congregation in Logansport; it was mainly composed of Irish laborers employed on the canal. A small frame chapel erected near the canal bank was used until a stone church was built in Logansport in 1839.[36]

The Catholic presence in Lafayette was apparently minimal during the 1830s before the Wabash and Erie Canal entered Tippecanoe County. Catholic activity in Lafayette increased with the arrival of Irish canal workers. In 1840 about fifteen Catholic families were living in Lafayette, and in response to their petition for regular visits by a missionary priest, Father Augustus Martin, Father John Claude Francois, and Father Lalumiere successively made trips to

Wedding dress of an Irish American in Indiana, 1845. Even in a new environment, many Irish immigrants retained cherished traditions.

Indiana Historical Society, R 0605

Lafayette. Mass was read in the homes of Frank Daily and James H. McKernan. Describing Catholic worship in the absence of a church structure in Lafayette, a local church historian, writing later in the century, reported: "Mass in those days was offered in the houses of different members of the congregation, and when they all assembled it was quite a gala day. Whilst the priest heard confessions in one room the women were preparing dinner in another. All who were present were expected to dine at the house where mass was said. The men assembled out of doors, discussing fluctuations of the currency. . . . Everyone kept open house in turn."[37]

There were twenty-five Catholic families in Lafayette in 1843, when Lafayette's first resident priest, Father Michael Clark, held services in a rented room in a building occupied by a religious bookstore. In response to a growing Catholic population, St. Mary and Martha Church was built in Lafayette in 1844.[38]

The appearance of Irish immigrants stimulated Catholic Church activity in towns on the National Road, including Richmond, Indianapolis, and Terre Haute during the 1832–46 period. In the 1830s traveling priests visited Richmond Catholics, some of whom were Irish (such as the O'Hara family), and said Mass in private homes. Father Michael O'Rourke occasionally made trips to Richmond during the early 1840s. Father O'Rourke was the resident priest at Dover in Dearborn County. Father John Ryan was Richmond's first resident priest. He organized a Richmond parish composed of Irish and German families and built St. Andrew Church in 1846. Mass was celebrated by missionary priests in the residences of Catholic families in Indianapolis (including those of Michael Shea and John O'Connor) prior to the opening of the first Catholic church in Indianapolis (Holy Cross) in 1840.[39]

Although a number of Catholics lived in Vigo County, there was only one Catholic resident of Terre Haute during the early 1830s when traveling priests occasionally visited the area. A few Terre Haute Catholics erected a church in 1838, when the National Road construction was nearing their town. The 1838–41 records of Terre Haute's St. Joseph Church show an increasing number of Irish family names, including Murphy, Byrne, Dugan, Cahill, and Kelly as well as some English and German names. Father Lalumiere became resident priest at Terre Haute in 1842. The largest group in his congregation was composed of the Irish with some Kentuckians (English stock) and Germans.[40] Describing the Terre Haute parish in 1845, one of Father Lalumiere's parishioners wrote, "We have but a small congregation [about sixty communicants] and they with few exceptions are very poor, living by daily labor of the hardest, and who can scarce spare time to practice their religious duties."[41]

There was comparable Catholic activity involving the Irish in towns and settlements near the Ohio River from 1832 through 1846. In Floyd County the old Irish Catholic settlement on Little Indian Creek (Lafayette Township) was enlarged by Irish and German newcomers during the 1830s. Father Louis Neyron (a Frenchman) brought about the replacement of the Catholic settlement's old log chapel. In 1837 a new brick building called St. Mary Church was erected on a hill overlooking the creek valley. Patrick Byrns and Patrick Duffey made the bricks for the building. These natives of Ireland were among the first settlers of the area. Also in Floyd County during the early 1830s, the New Albany Catholics attended St. Mary Church in Lafayette Township. New Albany Catholics also heard Mass said in private homes when a traveling priest visited their city. The augmentation of the local Catholic population led to the organization of the Holy Trinity Parish in New Albany and to the erection of a church building there (circa 1836). The members of the Holy Trinity Congregation had Irish, German, French, and English family names. The Irish names included McKenna, Dougherty, Mullin, Flannagan, McGuire, O'Brien, and Riley. In Dearborn County the old Catholic parish at Dover (Kelso Township) was still composed of Irish and English families. The Dover parish had grown enough by 1840 to justify the assignment of Father Conrad Schneiderjans as its first resident priest. Also, that growth prompted the replacement of the old log church with a new frame one. During 1842–46 Father Michael O'Rourke was assigned to St. John the Baptist Parish at Dover.[42]

The years 1846–60 formed another distinct period of Irish history in the state. Indiana was no longer in its pioneer phase; roads, canals, and railroads connected previously isolated communities in the state and prompted further urban and industrial growth. The Irish immigration to Indiana was much larger than in the past. While many natives of Ireland resided in rural areas of the state, the Irish foreign-born population became more urban in the decade before 1860.

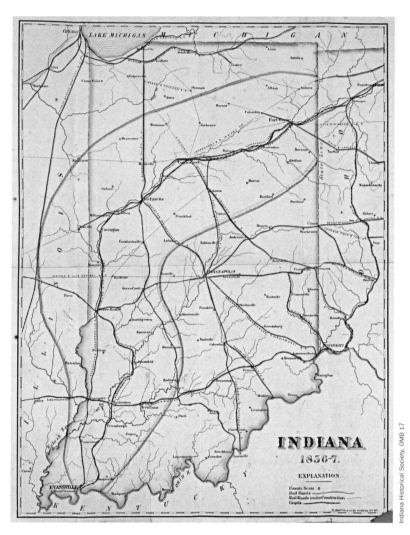

Irish immigrants contributed to the development of nineteenth-century Indiana transportation, working on both canal systems and railroad lines.

Several factors gave impetus to Irish immigration to Indiana after 1846. A terrible potato famine caused an exodus from Ireland during these years. In 1847 as the national economy was improving, the Indiana legislature refinanced the state debt in ways that permitted private companies to complete the construction of some canals begun earlier. Wabash and Erie Canal construction was resumed in earnest, the work being completed in 1853. This demand for labor again provided a motive for Irish construction workers to come to Indiana. The 1830s pattern of Irish life on the Wabash and Erie Canal was repeated in southern Indiana after 1846 when canal construction was in progress between Terre Haute, Washington, and Evansville. In the early 1850s the canal was under construction in Pike, Gibson, and Vanderburgh counties. Sixty-odd years later Gibson County witnesses to the canal work related their memories to the author of a county history. One observer stated:

> On these heavy works there was a large number of men, carts, and teams at work for nearly three years. . . . They had a very large plow on these works which the writer has seen drawn by eight yoke of heavy oxen. Shanties for the people and rough stables for the horses and oxen were scattered so thickly that it looked like a string town for many miles along the canal. . . . There were a hundred boarding shanties [on the canal line in] Gibson County. Some of these shanties were eighty feet long and would have bunks for as many as fifty boarders. . . . Nearly all of the people who lived near the works were Irish. They had no trouble getting all the whiskey they required.[43]

As in the past, canal work endangered the health of Irish laborers and caused many deaths. Unsanitary conditions in canal shantytowns fostered cholera epidemics. Hundreds of people died in a cholera outbreak on the canal south of Covington in 1849.[44] Recalling an extraordinarily high number of deaths in a cholera epidemic on the canal in Gibson County, a witness stated: "The stricken would die within three or four hours. On the old Potter farm . . . so many people were sick and dead that the canal people hired a cooper . . . to make boxes for coffins. . . . There was a general stampede from the works. Cold weather came, and work was resumed. There were three dead Irishmen found in a blacksmith shop . . . two miles north of Oakland City."[45]

The Irish came to Indiana to be employed on railroad lines constructed before 1860. Railroad construction was so extensive during the 1850s that all the state's larger cities had rail connections

Members of the St. Michael Church in Madison helped create this railroad cut for the Indianapolis and Madison Railroad.

St. Michael's Church, Madison, Indiana: A Pioneer Parish of Southern Indiana, 1817–1937 (Madison, IN: Abbey Press, 1937), 34.

by 1860. The first significant railroad in Indiana was completed in 1847; it linked Madison and Indianapolis. Many Irish immigrants came to Madison to work on the railroad there. Similarly Irish newcomers located in Indianapolis in consequence of railroad work. A group of Irish immigrants took residence in South Bend in 1851, after working on the construction of a railroad connecting Buffalo, South Bend, and Chicago. Another group of Irish families settled in South Bend later in the decade after finishing work on a railroad joining Philadelphia, South Bend, and Chicago. Irish

Catholic laborers were found in large construction camps along new rail lines in Indiana, where they received the support and guidance of traveling Catholic priests. For example, in 1853 or 1854 Father John Baptist Corbe gave the last rites to a sick Irish workman in a railroad construction camp in Vigo County where about two hundred Catholic families were living. Also, Father Patrick McDermott attended Catholic mission stations along the Evansville and Crawfordsville Railroad when it was under construction in the early 1850s.[46]

Irish workers contributed much to the building of roads, canals, and railroads in Indiana. These transportation improvements

TABLE A

INDIANA CENSUS OF POPULATION*

Year	Born in Ireland	Foreign Born	Total Population
1850	12,787	55,537	988,416
1860	24,495	118,184	1,350,428
1870	28,698	141,474	1,680,637
1880	25,741	144,178	1,978,301
1890	20,819	146,205	2,192,404
1900	16,306	142,121	2,516,462
1910	11,266	159,663	2,700,876
1920	7,271	150,868	2,930,390
1930	3,931	142,999	3,238,503
1940	2,657	110,631	3,427,796
1950	2,352	100,630	3,934,224
1960	1,673	93,202	4,662,498
1970	1,152	83,198	5,193,669
1980	825	101,802	5,490,224
1990	733	94,263	5,544,159
2000	845	186,534	6,080,485

*Based on United States Department of Commerce, Bureau of the Census, *Census of Population* for the years 1850–2000.

aided the state's population growth at midcentury by facilitating immigration into Indiana. During the 1850s the number of Irish immigrants in Indiana almost doubled, and the number of foreign-born in the state grew twofold. The number of Irish natives in Indiana increased from 12,787 in 1850 to 24,495 in 1860. Meanwhile, the Indiana foreign-born population grew from 55,537 to 118,184. Thus, Irish immigrants comprised 23 percent of the foreign-born in Indiana in 1850 and 21 percent of the state's foreign-born in 1860. It should be noted that the foreign-born were but a small proportion of the total population of Indiana, which was 988,416 in 1850 and 1,350,428 in 1860. Only 8.8 percent of the state's total population was foreign-born in 1860.[47]

Examinations of federal census records reveal that Irish immigrants became less concentrated in southern Indiana during the 1850s. While natives of Ireland were living in every Indiana county, the numbers of Irish immigrants were greatest in the southern reaches of the state in 1850. Many Irish canal and railroad laborers were working on construction projects in southern Indiana at midcentury. Further, the foreign-born were generally more heavily concentrated in southern Indiana because the state had been settled from south to north and because many early immigrants had come to Indiana via the Ohio River. A disproportionate percentage of the Irish lived in a few Indiana counties. The ten counties with the greatest numbers of persons born in Ireland contained 53 percent of the Irish immigrants in all of the state's ninety-two counties in 1850. Seven of these counties with high Irish populations in 1850 were in southern Indiana (Daviess, Dearborn, Floyd, Jefferson, Jennings, Pike, and Vanderburgh); two of them were in central Indiana (Marion and Tippecanoe); and one was in northern Indiana (Allen). In consequence of general demographic and economic trends, the distribution of Irish immigrants in Indiana began to shift northward during the 1850s. The 1860 census revealed that four of the ten Indiana counties with the greatest populations of persons born in Ireland were in the southern section (Dearborn, Floyd, Jefferson, and Vanderburgh); four were in the central section (Marion, Tippecanoe, Vigo, and Wayne); and two were in the northern section (Allen and La Porte). Irish population gains were greater in the state's central and northern counties during the 1850s than in its southern counties. During the same decade Irish immigrant populations actually declined in a few of the southern counties, including Daviess, Pike, and Jennings.[48]

Irish immigrants tended to locate in counties on new transportation routes in all sections of Indiana during the 1850s. The Wabash and Erie Canal, the Indianapolis and Madison Railroad, and the National Road passed through nine of the ten Indiana counties containing the greatest numbers of Irish immigrants in 1850 and 1860. Many Irish construction laborers eventually settled along transportation routes where they had worked. Some Irish newcomers probably purchased canal land at the bargain prices that the Wabash and Erie Canal trustees had advertised in their attempt to recruit immigrant workers. Other Irish construction workers did not settle near the canals, roads, or railroads they had built. Many of them were transients. In 1834 Father Badin advised against the erection of chapels at canal construction locations because Catholic workers were at such places only temporarily. There was an Irish exodus following the completion of canal building in Pike County, where the number of persons born in Ireland fell from 683 in 1850 to 35 in 1860. The number of Irish laborers who had worked on canals, roads, and railroads undoubtedly was not large enough to account entirely for the Irish population increase during the 1850s. Apparently, additional Irish immigrants were attracted to Indiana by the promise of economic opportunity, especially in the cities on new transportation lines. The transportation improvements fostered economic growth, creating employment opportunities for immigrants in these cities and providing the foreign-born with the means of accessing them. Irish population increases were especially great in counties with eco-

TABLE B

NUMBER OF PERSONS BORN IN IRELAND FOR TEN INDIANA COUNTIES WITH THE GREATEST IRISH FOREIGN-BORN POPULATIONS (GROUPED BY STATE REGIONS), 1850–1920*

Region and County	1850	1860	1870	1880	1890	1900	1910	1920
Northern								
Allen	406	697	982	1,030	843	598	449	292
Cass	—	—	963	732	616	479	298	164
Lake	—	—	—	—	505	573	729	908
La Porte	—	877	666	—	—	—	—	105
St. Joseph	—	—	—	618	636	551	466	345
Central								
Grant	—	—	—	—	—	371	200	—
Madison	—	—	—	—	—	478	259	160
Marion	492	1,748	3,760	4,064	4,127	4,009	3,383	2,488
Montgomery	—	—	626	—	—	—	—	—
Tippecanoe	917	1,645	1,926	1,238	959	636	395	189
Vigo	—	949	1,391	1,396	1,097	809	624	366
Wayne	—	884	956	852	593	427	247	131
Southern								
Clark	—	—	873	664	447	—	—	—
Daviess	838	—	—	—	—	—	—	—
Dearborn	813	866	—	—	—	—	—	—
Floyd	451	835	—	—	—	—	—	—
Jefferson	1,313	970	972	568	—	—	—	—
Jennings	367	—	—	—	—	—	—	—
Pike	683	—	—	—	—	—	—	—
Vanderburgh	498	730	—	534	424	—	—	—

*Based on United States Department of Commerce, Bureau of the Census, *Census of Population* for the years 1870–1920. Also, "1850 Census Foreign-Born for Indiana" (unpublished manuscript, Education Division, Indiana Historical Society, 1991); "1860 Census Foreign-Born for Indiana" (unpublished manuscript, Education Division, Indiana Historical Society, 1991).

nomically booming cities. For example, the Irish foreign-born populations of Marion County (Indianapolis) and Vigo County (Terre Haute) more than tripled between 1850 and 1860, when there was less than a doubling of the number of Irish immigrants in the state. Conversely, the Irish immigrant population of Jefferson County decreased by about one-quarter during the 1850s as that county's principal city (Madison) entered a period of economic decline.[49]

During the period 1816–60 most Irish immigrants in Indiana were located in rural areas, where they lived in villages or on farms. A demographic study revealed that in 1850 farming was the occupation of 53 percent of the Irish immigrants in northern Indiana, which was the most rural section of the state. Ninety-one percent of the state's total population was rural in 1860, when few Indiana counties had cities with populations of 2,500 or more. Thus, most Indiana counties with Irish immigrant populations were entirely rural in 1860.[50]

Nevertheless, in 1860 Indiana's Irish population was much more urban than the state's general population. Only 8.6 percent of the total state population was urban, that is, located in cities with minimum populations of 2,500. But at least one-third of the Irish foreign-born lived in urban places (8,685 of 24,495). Naturally, the proportion of the Irish living in cities was highest in Indiana counties with urban centers. For example, 93.5 percent of the natives of Ireland in Floyd County (New Albany) were urban dwellers (781 of 835). Irish immigrants were a comparatively urban people in all regions of the United States, especially in the Northeast where most Irish newcomers were concentrated.[51]

In some respects Irish urban experiences in Indiana reflected Irish life in major eastern cities before 1860. In New York City and Boston the great mass of Irish workers were in the lowest paying occupations, that is, unskilled labor for Irish men and domestic service for Irish women. Similarly, in South Bend during this period between one-half and two-thirds of Irish workingmen were

employed as laborers. In Terre Haute in 1860, 69 percent of foreign-born Irish workingmen and women were laborers (45 percent)
and domestic servants (24 percent). Irish immigrants accumulated
relatively little property in Indiana cities and elsewhere because so
many of them received low wages for unskilled work. In 1860 the
median values of personal and real property owned by Irish immigrants in South Bend were lower than the comparable figures for
other European immigrants in that city. Also, the average values of
real and personal property owned by Irish natives in Terre Haute
were found to be low in 1860. Indiana's urban and rural Irish immigrants had different statistical profiles regarding occupations and
property ownership. Relatively few of the rural Irish in the state were
employed in unskilled labor by midcentury. In 1850 only about 26
percent of Irish men were laborers in the largely rural counties of
northern Indiana. The remainder of the Irish in those twenty-one
counties was employed in agriculture, businesses, professions, and
skilled crafts. Irish immigrants in the latter occupations in all parts
of Indiana included persons who possessed surplus capital or craft
skills. Immigrants in this category either possessed financial assets
or skills upon arrival in the United States or acquired them after
entry into the country. Many Irish who came to Indiana during
1816–60 had lived in other states (chiefly in the Northeast) or in
Canada. Irish newcomers lacking capital and skills tended to locate
in Indiana cities that seemed to offer the best opportunities for
their advancement.[52]

In other respects there were great contrasts between the experiences of the urban Irish in Indiana and elsewhere. In Boston and
New York City impoverished Irish immigrants were housed poorly
in densely populated slum areas, where they were exposed to social
problems involving crime, ill health, and illiteracy. Undoubtedly,
population densities were comparatively low in immigrant residential areas of Indiana cities. The Irish in Indiana did not experience the intense social ills typical of eastern slum life. However,

they did not escape entirely social problems associated with poverty. For example, the Irish immigrants in Indiana had a high illiteracy rate, even in rural areas. In the counties of northern Indiana there were more illiterates among the natives of Ireland than in any other group in 1850.[53]

Many Irish women earned money working as domestic servants for affluent Indiana families.

Indiana Historical Society, P 0178

Also, the social life of the urban Irish in Indiana contrasted with that of the Irish in the East during the 1850s. There were differences in residential patterns and in organizational activities. The Irish in Indiana did not form great immigrant ghettos like those found in Boston. In Indiana the urban Irish were generally dispersed, although there were varying degrees of residential concentrations of the foreign-born Irish in the state's cities. In 1850 Irish immigrants resided in all five Lafayette wards, but 51 percent of Lafayette's Irish-born population lived in the city's first ward, and another 22 percent resided in its fifth ward. Natives of Ireland living in Terre Haute in 1860 were almost evenly distributed in that city's five wards, each of which contained less than one-quarter of the total Irish immigrant population. In 1860 foreign-born Irish men were evenly distributed in Madison's nine wards, but the concentrations of the Irish men were somewhat greater in wards 8–9 (south) and in wards 1–3 (north). Ethnic residential segregation was also weak in South Bend. But Irish residents of South Bend were especially found in the fourth ward (east side) and in the third ward (west side) in 1860.

Urban Irish immigrants were dispersed because they chose residences in close proximity to their workplaces. For instance, many Irish women lived in Terre Haute's second ward because it contained affluent neighborhoods where they were employed as domestic servants. Thus more female natives of Ireland resided in the second ward than in any other Terre Haute ward in 1860. In South Bend Irish employees of Notre Dame lived on the east side in the fourth ward, while Irish employees working for west-side factories and railroads resided in the third ward. The Irish laborers who were engaged in the construction of the railroad incline plane west of Madison took residence in the western part of Madison. Newcomers from Ireland in the urban East formed cultural institutions including churches, schools, and newspapers in efforts to maintain their Irish heritage. The Irish newcomers in Indiana had a similar cultural history before 1860, although they were evidently not active in establishing the kind of benevolent and fraternal organizations that formed much of the social life of Irish immigrants in eastern cities.[54]

As previously indicated, the urban and rural Irish in the state were much involved in the organization of Catholic parishes and in the erection of Catholic Church edifices between 1830 and 1860. Catholic congregations were initially composed of ethnic

St. Michael, a Catholic church in Madison, ca. 1937.

St. Michael's Church, Madison, Indiana, Indiana: A Pioneer Parish of Southern Indiana, 1817–1937 (Madison, IN: Abbey Press. 1937), inside front cover, 4.

mixtures, including Irish and German parishioners. After 1846 Catholic parishes in Indiana became more segregated along nationality lines. During the 1840s the German population increase was great enough to permit the formation of German-language churches. A predominantly Irish congregation remained in the initial Catholic church of a city when the German communicants withdrew to form a separate parish. This occurred in a number of Indiana cities. The phenomenon began in 1848 in Fort Wayne and Evansville, which had the largest German populations in the state. The parishioners of St. Michael Church of Madison became largely Irish after the founding of a German church in 1851. Likewise, chiefly Irish Catholic parishes were created in Lafayette in 1853 and in New Albany in 1854 when new German parishes were formed. In Indianapolis the Irish proportion of the St. John Congregation increased after St. Mary (German) was opened in 1858.[55]

Some Catholic parishes were principally Irish when they were organized in the 1850s. The Irish composed most of the congregation of northern Madison's St. Patrick Church, which was built near the Irish neighborhoods in that city. The Irish outnumbered the Germans in the congregation of South Bend's first Catholic church, which was opened on the city's east side in 1853. Initially known as St. Alexis, it was called St. Joseph after 1860. In 1859 the Irish on South Bend's west side founded St. Patrick Church. In 1860 a predominantly Irish parish appeared in Richmond when Irish communicants withdrew from the first Catholic church there and formed St. Mary Church.[56]

Indiana's Irish were involved in other cultural institutions as well. At least one parochial school was maintained in virtually every largely Irish Catholic parish in Indiana cities by 1860. Irish ethnic newspapers evidently were not published in Indiana before the Civil War, even though the *New York Irish-American* and other newspapers appeared elsewhere. Yet Irish immigrants were associated with Indiana newspapers. For example, John Dowling (born in Ballinrush, Ireland) was editor of the *Terre Haute Wabash Courier* during the 1830s.[57]

The Irish were active in Indiana politics and government during 1816–60. Irish immigrants soon became a factor in nineteenth-century party politics. Irish voters supported the Democratic Party, which adopted positions sympathetic to immigrants, in contrast to the Whig Party, which took nativist stands. The Democrats used their control of the 1850–51 state constitutional convention to ease voting requirements for immigrants. Three of the six foreign-born delegates to the constitutional convention were natives of Ireland. The 1851 state constitution stated that aliens could vote providing that they declared their intentions to become citizens and met a minimal residence requirement. During the 1850s many Irish aliens sought the franchise under these terms. A study of county naturalization records shows that three-fourths of the Irish aliens in Terre Haute who declared their intentions regarding citizenship during the decade did so in the general election years of 1854, 1856, and 1860. Also, in each instance most of these Irish men declared their citizenship intentions during the week preceding election day.[58]

Nativism and the Know-Nothing movement formed part of the background of Irish involvement in Indiana politics during the 1850s. Anti-Catholic attitudes were common in early nineteenth-century Indiana, and such attitudes intensified as the state's Catholic population increased and as attacks were made on the Catholic Church. Stories alleging immorality in Catholic convents were circulated. In 1853 large crowds in Indianapolis heard Father Alessandro Gavazzi, a defrocked priest, accuse the church in Rome of possessing inordinate power, criticize Catholic education, and recall the Inquisition. Similarly, in 1853 anti-Catholic columns appeared in the *Terre Haute Wabash Courier*. The demise of the Whig Party in the first third of the decade left a vacuum that was partially filled in 1854 with the emergence of the anti-Catholic Know-Nothing political movement. The Know-Nothings supported severe naturalization laws and the restriction that only natives of the United States be eligible for office.[59] Nativists saw the Democrats as the Catholic immigrant party. A writer in the *Terre Haute Daily Wabash Express*, who generally regarded Democrats as "riff raff," stated: "Perhaps there never was a political gathering in this county [Vigo] which partook so much of Irish elements as the so-called Democratic meeting which met at City Hall on Sat. Eve. There were about 300 persons present and . . . there were not 40 native born citizens there."[60]

At the height of the Know-Nothing movement Catholics were harassed in some cities. Nativist political issues sometimes led to violence; for example, in Gibson County there were fights between native and Irish men. Some election-day riots involved nativists and Irish in 1854. The Republican Party, which was formed at mid-decade, did not reject Know-Nothingism and soon began to absorb the nativist vote. Meanwhile, the Democratic Party roundly condemned nativism. Know-Nothings and Republicans accused Democrats of purchasing the votes of Irish immigrants and encouraging Irish men to vote repeatedly at elections. Indeed, each party charged the other with vote fraud in the 1856 election. After Democratic successes in the latter election the Know-Nothing faction died, and the Republican Party repudiated nativism. However, in 1858 the Republican platform did not advocate religious liberty, and, although the Republican ticket carried an Irish Protestant, it did not include a Catholic.[61]

Irish immigrants were elected to Democratic Party positions and to public offices in Indiana before 1860. Democrat Patrick M. Brett (born county Tipperary) was Daviess County auditor (1841–44). William Stewart was Marion County clerk (1850–56) and secretary of the Democratic National Convention in 1852. Cornelius O'Brien (born in county Kilkenny) was Dearborn County clerk (1851–56) and delegate to the Democratic National Convention in 1856. At least twenty-five natives of Ireland were among the 1,513 legislators who served in the Indiana General Assembly from 1816 to 1850. Most of the foreign-born Irish legislators were Ulstermen; only nine Catholics were numbered among all the legislators during that period.[62]

Irish immigrants were interested in public affairs abroad as well as at home in the years before the Civil War. Many of Indiana's Irish newcomers were concerned about events in Ireland and were solicitous about the welfare of Ireland's people. The Irish in Indiana took steps to aid Ireland during the time of its terrible potato famine. The Committee for Irish Relief formed in Terre Haute in 1846. It collected $1,441.65, which was sent to Ireland in 1847. Also in 1847, $1,200 for famine relief was raised in Fort Wayne through the efforts of Irish immigrants who organized a public meeting at the courthouse, held a dinner at a public house, and made appeals in local churches. Corn was shipped from Madison to Ireland during the famine. Undoubtedly, the Irish in Indiana had warm feelings for the land of their birth, and some expressed these sentiments. John Ford and Martin Flanagan (county Galway natives) were the first residents of a farming community in Bartholomew County (near Columbus). Sweet Ireland was the name they gave to the settlement.[63]

The Irish newcomers to Indiana in 1832–60 joined a state early in its transition from a pioneer stage of socioeconomic life to a modern society. Irish immigrants before 1860 were involved in basic trends that would eventually shape life in the coming modern age—immigration, urbanization, and industrialization. Indiana became an urban industrial state by 1920 under the impact of these developments, which accelerated after 1860. Irish immigrants in the period 1860–1920 contributed to these trends, which in turn changed their lives in Indiana.

3. | Natives of Ireland and Urban Community Building: *1860–1920*

THE YEARS 1860–1920 FORMED ANOTHER DISTINCT period in the history of the Irish in Indiana. By 1920 Indiana's population was predominantly urban, and its economy was diversified with modern industry and agriculture. The number of Irish immigrants in Indiana was greater during this time than ever before or after. Irish newcomers were among the builders of modern Indiana. Irish workers were employed in railroad construction, which created a railroad network connecting the state's markets. Irish immigrants enlarged an expanding labor pool, which was fundamental to the acceleration of industrialization in the state. The disproportionate number of Irish immigrants who located in cities swelled Indiana's urban population. Also, the Irish community in Indiana was most evident as an ethnic group during the period 1860–1920. As their numbers increased, the Irish were further identified with ethnic cultural institutions. The social identity of the Irish community was defined by its ethnic residential patterns and by its new ethnic organizations.

Natives of Ireland remained prominent in Irish life in Indiana from 1860 to 1920. The Irish immigrant population of Indiana grew during the 1860s and rose to its highest number (28,698) in 1870. The size of the foreign-born Irish population in Indiana declined during the 1870s, and this trend continued through the remainder of the period as the number of Indiana residents who had been born in Ireland fell to 25,741 in 1880, to 20,819 in 1890, to 16,306 in 1900, to 11,266 in 1910, and to 7,271 in 1920. The smaller numbers of Irish immigrants in Indiana after 1870 reflected a late nineteenth-century change in the country's immigration pattern in which the national origin of most immigrants shifted from the countries of northern and western Europe to those of southern and eastern Europe. By 1910 there were more foreign-born Hungarian and Polish peoples in Indiana than Irish and English. Although the state's Irish foreign-born population declined after 1870, Irish immigration to Indiana was comparatively large through the end of the century, and Irish newcomers were influential. More than 20,000 Irish immigrants lived in Indiana from 1870 through 1890. The Irish immigrant population in Indiana remained greater than it was in 1850 until after 1900.[1]

The Irish remained widely distributed in Indiana. As late as 1920 at least a few Irish immigrants lived in every county of the state, excepting Warrick. While in the earlier period Irish immigrants had been mostly concentrated in the southern section of Indiana, Irish newcomers arriving after 1860 were more often found in the state's central and northern sections. After 1860 few of the ten Indiana counties with the greatest numbers of persons born in Ireland were located in the southern third of Indiana. In 1870 three of the counties with high Irish populations were in northern Indiana (Allen, Cass, and La Porte); five of them were in central Indiana (Marion, Montgomery, Tippecanoe, Vigo, and Wayne); and two were in southern Indiana (Clark and Jefferson). In 1900 four of the ten Indiana counties with the greatest populations of persons born in Ireland were in the northern section of the state (Allen, Cass, Lake, and St. Joseph); and six of them were in the central section (Grant, Madison, Marion, Tippecanoe, Vigo, and Wayne). The northward movement of the foreign-born Irish population was part of a larger late nineteenth century and early twentieth century phenomenon involving the growth of industries and urban populations in the central and northern counties of Indiana.[2]

The foreign-born Irish population of the 1860–1920 period was still concentrated in the Indiana counties containing cities with good transportation connections, expanding populations, and industries. For example, in 1900 six of the ten counties with the highest numbers of Irish immigrants were on the old Wabash and Erie Canal line and on the National Road (Allen, Cass, Marion, Tippecanoe, Vigo, and Wayne). More significant, these six counties contained expanding urban and industrial centers on railroad lines built in the latter half of the nineteenth century. Four of the ten counties with the greatest numbers of Irish newcomers also contained growing industrial cities on railroads constructed during the same era (Grant, Madison, Lake, and St. Joseph). Irish immigrants were attracted by the economic opportunities found in Indiana towns and cities that prospered following railroad building.[3]

While many of the Irish lived in rural areas of the state, Irish immigrants in Indiana became increasingly urban during 1860–1920. The rural Irish were sometimes found in Catholic farming areas such as the old Catholic Settlement on Little Indian Creek in Lafayette Township, Floyd County. Small Irish concentrations could be found in many towns, including Cannelton (Perry County), whose cotton mills employed Irish workers in the late nineteenth century. Yet a disproportionate number of the Irish lived in cities. The Irish immigrants were more urban than Indiana's general population throughout the period. Thus in 1920, 71.8 percent of the Irish foreign-born were urban, while that figure was only 50.6 percent for the total state population.[4]

The Irish were heavily employed in factory and construction work in Indiana cities after 1860. In some respects the employment experiences of the Irish who came to Indiana in the late nineteenth century were different from those of the Irish who entered the state before the Civil War. Earlier, the urban Irish were restricted largely to low-paying unskilled jobs. But a study of the 1880 census in South Bend found that only 23 percent of the Irish were common laborers while 68 percent were factory employees or skilled workers, and 8 percent were in businesses and professions. The Irish also worked in factories elsewhere; for example, in Madison a native of Ireland owned a starch factory that employed Irish immigrants. The Starch Works, located on the near south side of Indianapolis, employed Irish women. As in the past, Irish men were hired as construction workers. Irish workmen were employed in the erection of Union Station in Indianapolis and in the construction of the University of Notre Dame campus. The occupations and income of urban Irish put them near the bottom of the economic ladder, and their upward economic mobility was difficult. Although they had made gains in property ownership, the Irish in South Bend still owned less personal and real property than other European immigrant groups there in 1870.[5]

Indiana's Irish community experienced its greatest visibility during 1860–1920. In the late nineteenth century Irish society in Indiana was more sharply defined than it had been before 1860. Irish residential areas in cities were more identifiable than before. At least in some instances, the urban Irish became more residentially segregated in Indiana than in the past. Even so, they did not form exclusively Irish neighborhoods. The residential segregation of the Irish increased in the third and fourth wards of South Bend from 1870 to 1880. The Irish district in the fourth ward was on the east side near Water Street between Hill Street and St. Joseph Church. The Irish neighborhood in the third ward was on the west side near the railroad tracks and in the vicinity of St. Patrick Church. Irish immigrants who had arrived before 1870 remained in these South Bend neighborhoods, where newcomers from Ireland joined them in the 1870s. By 1880 notable concentrations of the Irish had developed in these South Bend wards through the accretion of immigrants from Ireland during a period covering more than two decades.

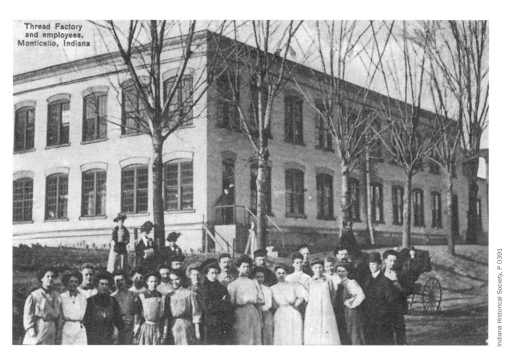

Thread Factory and employees, Monticello, Indiana

Indiana Historical Society, P 0391

Many Irish women were employed in factories such as this thread factory in Monticello, Indiana, in the early 1900s.

Predominantly Irish urban neighborhoods were sometimes identified by nicknames with ethnic connotations. The fourth ward Irish neighborhood in South Bend was nicknamed "Dublin." Irish neighborhoods that formed in other cities during the late nineteenth century had identities sharp enough to be remembered during the 1930s by people interviewed in a study of the Irish in Indiana made by the Federal Writers' Project. "Irish Town" in the southwest section of Fort Wayne was remembered by Patrick Murphy in the 1930s as he recalled his arrival in Fort Wayne in 1880. The Federal Writers' Project records noted "Irish Hollow" in Madison. Also, "Bog Hollow" of New Albany was recalled as an Irish settlement in an area resembling the bogs of Ireland; it was located between the Southern Railroad and the Ohio River. "Irish Hill" in Indianapolis was located south of Washington Street and west of Shelby Street.

Mustering out roll for William Flynn, member of the 35th Regiment,
Indiana's first Irish regiment in the Civil War.

Ninety percent of the Irish in Marion County once lived on "Irish
Hill," according to the Federal Writers' Project.[6]

Public awareness of Irish society in Indiana was raised as a variety of Irish organizations appeared in the state for the first time
after 1860. Two Irish regiments were formed in Indiana during the
Civil War. They were among several Indiana military units that were

recruited chiefly along nationality lines in the 1860s. The Thirty-fifth Regiment was the first Irish regiment. It was commanded by Col. John C. Walker. His troops wore green hats signifying their Irish identity. After mustering in December 11, 1861, the Thirty-fifth was sent to Kentucky and then to Tennessee. The Sixty-first Regiment was the second Irish regiment, and it was consolidated with the Thirty-fifth in Nashville. The enlarged Irish regiment participated in military action in Kentucky in the battle of Perryville (October 8, 1862) and in Tennessee in a skirmish at Dobbin's Ford (December 9, 1862) where five of its members were killed and thirty-five wounded. Later under Gen. William Rosecrans, the Thirty-fifth participated in the Battle of Stones River where twenty-nine members were killed and seventy-two wounded. It also suffered heavy losses in the Battle of Chickamauga (September 19–20, 1863). After re-enlistment and furlough in the winter of 1863–64, the Thirty-fifth returned to active duty as part of the Second Brigade of the First Division of Fourth Corps and was tested again. At Kennesaw Mountain regimental losses totaled eleven killed and fifty-four wounded. The Thirty-fifth entered Atlanta on September 9, 1864. Then, the Irish regiment marched with the Fourth Corps in pursuit of retreating Confederates. Later it was assigned to Franklin, Tennessee, engaging in action there and in the battle of Nashville. In June 1865 the Thirty-fifth was sent to Texas where it was mustered out in September. A public reception for the Irish regiment was held on the Statehouse grounds in Indianapolis on October 21, 1865.[7]

The Irish formed benevolent, fraternal, temperance, military, and musical organizations in Indiana during the latter decades of the nineteenth century. While they often had multiple purposes, all these associations met the Irish immigrants' need for companionship with others who shared their immigrant experiences and cultural heritage. Most of these organizations were founded in the 1870s and 1880s. The benevolent associations were established on the principle of mutual aid and typically provided benefits when members suffered illness or death. The United Irish Benevolent Association was organized in Indianapolis in 1870. According to its constitution, the aims of the association were to provide benevolence and "to promote the social welfare of Irish citizens; to create a fraternity of sympathy, and identity of interest, and a union of power among them."[8] Its membership was limited to persons of Irish birth or ancestry who were between the ages of eighteen and fifty and free of any physical infirmities likely to shorten life. The association had 150 members in its first year of existence. The United Irish Society existed in Indianapolis in the 1870s and in the 1880s. The St. Patrick's Temperance Benevolent Society appeared in Indianapolis in the 1870s, while the St. Patrick's Benevolent Society did so in the 1880s. The Hibernian Benevolent Society was active in Terre Haute between 1857 and 1917. The Young Men's Hibernian Society in Lafayette was a branch of the Irish Catholic Benevolent Union; it had 15 members when it was established in 1871 and 107 members in 1888. The Irish Catholic Benevolent Association was meeting in Fort Wayne in 1874. The Catholic Hibernian Benevolent Society of Evansville had 60 members in 1874 when it was established; it was still active in 1892. The Father Matthew Total Abstinence and Benevolent Society was founded in Logansport in 1870; it was still meeting in 1886.[9]

The Ancient Order of Hibernians (AOH) was one of the larger and more enduring of the Irish organizations formed in Indiana after 1860. It claimed antecedents in a fourteenth-century Irish society with ties to St. Patrick. Established in the United States in 1836, the AOH was reorganized as a nationwide association in 1871. Membership was restricted to natives of Ireland until 1884 when persons of Irish ancestry were also admitted to the order. The membership policy change was influenced by a decline in emigration from Ireland. In the order's early years the Hibernians were essentially a fraternal association interested in the celebration of St. Patrick's Day. Subsequently the order broadened its program to include provision of insurance benefits, advocacy of Irish independence, and criticism of the stage Irishman. The first AOH division in Indiana was founded in Knightsville (Clay County) in 1871. It was organized by Thomas McGovern, who became the first state delegate. Units of the AOH were founded in Indianapolis in 1873, in Terre Haute in 1879, in Lafayette and Logansport in 1883, in South Bend in 1885, and in other cities. The AOH was active in Indiana cities through the end of the century. Also, the Hibernians were organized at the county and state levels in Indiana. AOH offices included county delegate and state president. For example, John W. McGreevy of Logansport was elected state president in 1884 and reelected in 1886.[10]

Listings in city directories revealed varying levels of Hibernian activity in Indianapolis from 1873 to 1900. An increasing interest in the AOH in Indianapolis during the 1870s was indicated by the growing number of its lodges there. In 1874 the local AOH was composed of Lodge numbers 1 and 2, each holding weekly meetings. The AOH was designated as a benevolent organization for the first time in 1878. Meanwhile it continued to expand, and by 1879 six AOH lodges met either weekly or bimonthly. During the 1870s each lodge listed a president and a secretary. AOH county officers were named for the first time in 1879. The countywide organization of the AOH in Marion County was broadened in the early 1880s as the office of AOH county treasurer was added to the offices of county delegate and county secretary. However, AOH activity declined in Indianapolis during the 1880s, when there were as few as two AOH lodges. The lodges met bimonthly, which was less frequently than in the past. Undoubtedly, the decline of the AOH in the 1880s involved membership losses to other Irish organizations founded in Indianapolis during the decade. The other associations did not survive the 1880s, and Hibernian activity increased again from 1890 to 1900. The number of AOH lodges in Indianapolis grew from three in 1889 to six by the end of the century. In 1898 the Indianapolis AOH listed a county headquarters in St. John's Hall and a county organization composed of the offices of president, secretary, and treasurer.[11]

Irish women's organizations were founded in Indiana after 1860. Such groups included the Maids of Erin, which appeared in Indianapolis in 1876. The Sodality Society of the Church of the Assumption in Evansville was established in 1878. Alice Doyle, N. Haney, and Mary Shea were the officers of this society for young ladies in 1885. Also, local female units of the Ancient Order of Hibernians were organized

Irish women celebrated their heritage through ethnic organizations such as this women's auxiliary of the Ancient Order of Hibernians, 1904.

in Indiana cities including Fort Wayne and Terre Haute. AOH Ladies' Auxiliaries numbers 1 and 2 met in Terre Haute in 1904 and remained active through 1920. These Terre Haute auxiliaries held twice-monthly meetings in St. Joseph and St. Ann churches, respectively. Each of these associations was headed by a president, secretary, and treasurer. The female Hibernians in Terre Haute also had a county organization with offices of president, secretary, and treasurer.[12]

Various other Irish organizations in Indiana included fraternal orders such as the Friendly Sons of St. Patrick, founded in Indianapolis in 1881, and the Knights of Erin, located in Terre Haute in 1882. The Emmet Guards, a military association of Irish men, was active in Indianapolis at various times from 1870 through 1890. The Emmet Guard Band marched in Indianapolis in the early 1890s. Also, the Hibernian Rifles appeared in Indianapolis in 1898. Irish temperance groups in the state included the St. Patrick Total Abstinence Society of Indianapolis, which was active in 1878 and remained so through 1890. The St. Joseph Total Abstinence Society of Terre Haute met from 1879 through the end of the century.[13]

St. John Church in Indianapolis served as a gathering place for the Irish community.

Indiana Historical Society, P 0130

A great deal of the social life of Indiana's Irish was related to the Catholic Church. As indicated previously, many Irish ethnic organizations had ties with churches in Catholic parishes that were chiefly Irish. In addition, the Irish joined Catholic associations founded in

Indiana in the late nineteenth century. These groups included the Knights of Father Matthew, the Catholic Knights of America, and the Knights of Columbus. The significant social role of the Catholic Church was exemplified by St. John Church in Indianapolis, which during the period 1870–1900 sponsored activities such as lectures, cultural entertainments, lawn festivals, card parties, and weekend retreats.[14]

In the late nineteenth century, the Irish in Indiana observed St. Patrick's Day as an occasion for religious observance and as a day of great celebration. The AOH often took the lead in St. Patrick's Day celebrations in Indiana after 1871. Nevertheless, the Irish Delegate Assembly, which met regularly in Indianapolis, invited representatives of Irish associations from all across the state to attend an Indianapolis meeting on St. Patrick's Day in 1879. The events included a parade and an address, "The Social Mission of the Irish Race," by the Most Reverend Bishop Francis Silas Chatard, bishop of Indianapolis. "There was always a big celebration on St. Patrick's day and a dance at night," according to Irish immigrant Patrick Murphy who lived in Fort Wayne during the 1880s.[15] Murphy also recalled that the Irish in Fort Wayne regularly held dances on Saturday and Sunday nights. Old Irish dances including reels, jigs, hornpipes, and breakdowns were sometimes performed. According to Murphy, at times doors were taken off hinges and placed on carpeted floors so that the dancers would have a hard surface for dancing the hornpipe. Such dances and parties were sometimes held in the homes of the Irish. In early twentieth-century Indianapolis, "Greenhorn" parties to welcome immigrants were held in Irish homes, where rugs were rolled up for dancing.[16]

The Irish in Indiana were identified with cultural institutions as well as with social organizations during the period 1860–1920. Additional predominantly Irish Catholic congregations were created. Catholic parishes had begun to divide along ethnic lines before 1860, and this trend continued afterward. In Jeffersonville the

English-speaking Catholics, who were largely Irish, separated from the German parishioners of St. Anthony and formed the congregation of St. Augustine, which was opened in time to be blessed on St. Patrick's Day in 1868. St. Joseph's congregation in Terre Haute became mainly Irish in 1865 when German communicants formed St. Benedict Parish. In 1869 there was an increase in the Irish proportion of the congregation of St. Vincent de Paul Church in Logansport when German communicants formed a parish. In South Bend St. Patrick's congregation remained predominantly Irish after 1870, although it was composed of persons of different nationalities. Polish people living in South Bend attended St. Patrick until 1877 when they formed their own parish. Similarly, some of the Belgians residing in South Bend attended St. Patrick for two decades before they founded their own parish in 1898. Chiefly Irish congregations were formed in new Catholic churches constructed in urban neighborhoods where Irish newcomers settled in greater numbers after 1860. For example, in 1865 St. Patrick (initially St. Peter) Church of Indianapolis was erected at the terminus of Virginia Avenue, which was near the eastern edge of the city's south-side Irish community. Parochial schools that were started in predominantly Irish parishes before 1860 still offered Catholic education, and new ones were opened during this period. For instance, a school was erected in the Church of the Assumption Parish of Evansville in 1881. The list of the leading promoters of the Assumption school contained many Irish names including Patrick Raleigh, Michael Gorman, Joseph Dillon, C. J. Murphy, Eugene McGrath, John J. Nolan, Charles McCarthy, and John McDonough.[17]

As in the era before 1860, the press was not a cultural institution developed by and for the Irish in Indiana before 1920. Undoubtedly, the Irish read the daily newspapers and publications of the Catholic press. Nevertheless, Irish individuals were involved in newspaper publications in the state. The *Indianapolis Western Citizen*, 1876–84, was published by Thomas McSheey who was a native

Irish immigrants were involved in newspaper publications throughout Indiana.

of county Kerry, Ireland. John F. Joyce (Irish ancestry) held positions as copyboy, reporter, and editor of the *Terre Haute Gazette*, 1876–1906. Gabriel Summers (Irish ancestry) published the *South Bend News*, the *South Bend Times*, and, after a merger, the *South Bend News-Times*, 1908–20. Also, Joseph Patrick O'Mahony published the *Indiana Catholic* in the World War I period.[18]

Changes in Irish demographic history in Indiana became increasingly evident after the turn of the century. Some Irish neighborhoods began to show signs of change by 1920; however, in many places urban Irish residential patterns were still typical of the late nineteenth century. The old-style residential pattern was found in the relatively new city of Gary where 57 percent of the Irish immigrants were located in two of that city's ten wards (the first and the seventh) in 1920. The greatest concentrations of Irish immigrants in South Bend were still in the third and fourth wards; however, their numbers were much smaller than in the past. The nineteenth-century-style residential segregation of the Irish began to decline. By 1920 indications of increasing geographical mobility among the Irish began to appear. A movement of the Irish out of their old east-side and west-side South Bend neighborhoods began in 1915. Undoubtedly, many of the Irish leaving those South Bend areas were not of the immigrant generation. Also, the population of St. John Parish in Indianapolis was declining by 1915. Families moved away as the city encroached upon the old Irish residential areas. No Indianapolis ward held more than 15 percent of the city's Irish-born population in 1920.[19]

The number of foreign-born Irish in Indiana was decreasing while the number of persons of Irish ancestry born in the United States was increasing. The Irish immigrant population of Indiana fell from 16,306 in 1900 to 7,271 in 1920. During those decades the number of persons born in Ireland declined in every Indiana county but one. Natives of Ireland increased in Lake County as immigrants were attracted by Gary's industrial expansion during the opening decades of the century. Meanwhile, persons of Irish parentage formed a larger proportion of Indiana's Irish population; there were more than twice as many persons of Irish stock as there were natives of Ireland in 1910. Specifically, 24,556 persons in Indiana reported that both of their parents were born in Ireland, while only 11,266 people in Indiana indicated that they were natives of Ireland. The Irish made up 10 percent of the persons of foreign parentage in Indiana in 1920.[20]

Irish ethnic associations in Indiana began to fade during 1900–20 as the state's Irish immigrant population fell. The ethnic organizations were fewer in number and variety. The Irish benevolent societies tended to disband earlier than the Irish fraternal associations. The Hibernians were still organized in Fort Wayne in 1907 and in Logansport in 1913. The Hibernian units in Terre Haute and Indianapolis survived through 1920.[21]

Most of the Irish living in Indiana and elsewhere in the nation moved slowly upward on the path of economic advancement in the late nineteenth century. The Irish in Indiana moved further in that direction after 1900 as the state's Irish-stock population grew. Yet at the beginning of the century many Irish were still tied to relatively low-paying jobs in Indiana. Many of the Irish across the nation experienced poverty and its attendant social problems at this time. For instance, according to a federal report in 1901 the Irish had the greatest proportion of inmates in all charitable and penal institutions in the United States. These conditions were reflected in Indiana, although not as severely as elsewhere. Thus, the Irish were disproportionately represented in the Indiana state prison population. In 1902 there were ninety-three foreign-born state prison inmates including forty-eight Irish, twenty-seven Germans, and seven English. Nevertheless, by World War I the Irish in Indiana were typically hard-working employees in blue-collar occupations in the state's factories and skilled crafts.[22]

A number of the Irish were employed in the state's businesses and professions before World War I. For example, many Irish men started construction companies. In 1895 Daniel Foley founded the American Construction Company, which built streets and bridges. Foley was a native of county Kerry, Ireland, and a resident of Indianapolis. Also, the Irish were involved in grocery, drugstore, furniture, saloon, hotel, manufacturing, and other businesses in Indiana. Irish entrepreneurs in Indianapolis included Michael O'Connor, the owner of a wholesale grocery firm, and William J. Mooney, the co-owner of a wholesale drug company. Irish-owned furniture stores in Indianapolis included G. P. McGoughall and Son, Madden Furniture, and Michael Clune's firm. Mary Kennedy (the daughter of an

Indiana Historical Society, P 0130

Samuel Kingan brought his meatpacking plant from Northern Ireland to Indianapolis in 1862, where it continued in business until 1966. The Irish made up a large portion of Kingan's workforce.

Irish immigrant) purchased a drugstore in Lawrenceburg after her graduation from pharmacy college in 1905. Stephen J. Hannagan (whose parents were born in Ireland) bought a saloon in Lafayette after he had worked a number of years in local factories. Patrick McCormick, born in county Limerick, Ireland, owned the St. Denis Hotel in Columbus. Gabriel Summers (Irish ancestry) was the president of the South Bend Iron Bed Company, a manufacturing firm. The professions entered by the Irish in Indiana included law, teaching, medicine, and the clergy. For example, Dr. E. J. Brennan (born in Kilkenny, Ireland) was a staff member of the Indianapolis City Hospital. Brennan was also on the faculty of the Central College of Physicians and Surgeons and a member of the Indianapolis Board of Health in the late nineteenth century.[23]

The Catholic Church and politics served as avenues of social advancement for the Irish in America before 1920. The hierarchy of the Catholic Church in America was dominated by the Irish. In Indiana, however, the Catholic prelates were of French and German origin. Nevertheless, an Indiana native of Irish ancestry, the Reverend Denis O'Donoghue, was appointed auxiliary bishop of the Indianapolis diocese in 1900 and then named bishop of Louisville in 1910. Other Irish men and women in Indiana devoted their lives to the Catholic Church. Many Irish priests were assigned to Catholic parishes in Indiana during 1860–1920. Some were natives of Ireland, for example, Father Hugh O'Neill (county Waterford) and Father Patrick McDermott (county Roscommon). They served St. Patrick's parish in Indianapolis between 1868 and 1885. Many of the Irish women teaching in Indiana were on Catholic parochial school faculties. Politics enhanced the careers of Irish lawyers in Indiana. A large proportion of the Indiana legislators of Irish ancestry were attorneys. Also, the Irish who were successful in business in Indiana were often involved in politics. Most of those listed herein as examples of the Irish in businesses were also active in politics. Some Irish men with political connections became policemen and firemen in Indiana cities, and some of them became chiefs. John Kennedy and James J. Daugherty were Terre Haute fire chiefs in 1894 and 1900, respectively.[24]

The Irish were a significant force in American urban politics during 1860–1920. Indiana's Irish were not numerous enough to constitute the kind of strong voting blocs that strengthened the hands of Irish politicos elsewhere. However, many of Indiana's Irish politicians possessed the skills requisite for political success. The state's Irish voters were identified with the Democratic Party, and Irish candidates for office were usually on the Democratic ticket in Indiana. Irish politicians played important roles in Democratic Party leadership. Thomas Taggart of Indianapolis was a powerful figure in state and national Democratic Party affairs. Taggart was Democratic state

Indiana State Library Picture Collection

Thomas Taggart stands behind President Theodore Roosevelt (at the far left in the insert) at the Indianapolis residence of Vice President Charles Fairbanks, 1907.

Indiana State Library Photograph Collection

chairman (1892–94) and Democratic National Committee chairman (1904–08). In addition, he was a member of the party's national committee (1900–12) and a delegate to all of its national conventions from 1900 to 1924. Taggart worked in association with William Hunter O'Brien, who was born in Lawrenceburg. O'Brien was chairman of the Democratic State Central Committee, treasurer of the Democratic National Committee (1908), and delegate to Democratic national conventions in 1900, 1904, 1916, and 1920. Also, O'Brien was mayor of Lawrenceburg (1885–94, 1898–1902), state senator (1903, 1905), and auditor of the state (1911–15).[25]

Taggart and O'Brien were Protestants. Taggart was a native of county Monaghan in northern Ireland. O'Brien (whose father was born in county Kilkenny) followed his mother (Jane Hunter O'Brien) into the Methodist Church. Also, five Protestants of Irish ancestry were elected mayor in Indianapolis during 1860–1900. Republicans Daniel McCauley and John Caven were mayors of Indianapolis in the 1860s and 1870s. Thomas Mitchell, a Democrat, was

Timothy Edward Howard served on the Indiana Supreme Court from 1893 to 1899.

Indiana Supreme Court

elected mayor of Indianapolis in 1873. Democrats Thomas L. Sullivan and Thomas Taggart were Indianapolis mayors in the 1880s, 1890s, and early 1900s.[26]

There was a marked increase in the involvement of Irish Catholics in Indiana politics and government from 1860 to 1920. Usually running as Democrats, they were elected to a great variety of offices during that period. Irish Catholic Democrats held various offices in municipal government. David J. Hefron was mayor of Washington (1871–75). Patrick H. McCormick (born in Ireland) was mayor of Columbus before 1900, and Thomas W. O'Connor was mayor of

Monticello (1909–13). Irish Catholic Democrats on town and city councils included Timothy E. Howard, South Bend council (1878–84); Michael H. Farrell, Indianapolis board of aldermen (1889–91); and Stephen J. Hannagan, Lafayette council (1896–1910). John C. Lawler served three terms on the Salem council before 1900. John B. Kennedy (born in county Kilkenny) was on the Lawrenceburg council before 1912. Irish Catholic Democrats in other municipal offices included Charles McKenna (born in Ireland), who was elected street commissioner of New Albany in 1869; James Deery, elected Indianapolis city clerk in 1883; and Michael Sweeney, Jasper city marshal for four terms before 1900. John Francis McHugh was Lafayette city attorney (1889–95), and Michael Maloney was appointed postmaster of Aurora in 1913.[27]

Irish Catholic Democrats held many Indiana county positions during the 1860–1920 years. For example, John W. McGreevy was elected Cass County attorney in 1885, and Thomas Hanlon of county Clare, Ireland, was Floyd County auditor (1875–83, 1899–1908). John Sweeney of county Cork, Ireland, was Perry County sheriff (1878–80), and John F. Joyce was Vigo County clerk (1909–17).[28] Meanwhile, Irish Catholic Democrats were also elected to state offices in Indiana, including Matthew L. Brett of Washington, state treasurer (1863–65); James H. Rice of New Albany, state auditor (1883–87); Timothy E. Howard of South Bend, state supreme court judge (1893–99); and Joseph H. Shea of Seymour, judge of the fortieth circuit (1907–12) and judge of the state appellate court (1913–16).[29]

Justin Walsh, in *The Centennial History of the Indiana General Assembly, 1816–1978*, found that many Irish candidates were elected to the Indiana General Assembly after 1860. There were twenty-two natives of Ireland among the 1,966 members of the General Assembly during 1850–90. The 1,712 members of the General Assembly during 1890–1930 era included at least 125 legislators of Irish ancestry (five of whom were natives of Ireland). The Irish comprised many of the Catholic members of the legislature whose numbers rose from thirty-three during 1851–89 to ninety-three during 1891–1929. In a study of Indiana legislators of the 1896–1920 era, Philip R. VanderMeer found that the proportion of foreign-born Irish lawmakers in the legislature was about the same as the percentage of the foreign-born Irish in the total population. Also, VanderMeer noted that 85 percent of the lawmakers of Irish parentage were Democratic. Moreover, he reported that all of the Catholic legislators of Irish parentage were Democrats.[30]

The Irish in Indiana were interested in political issues concerning Ireland as well as in American politics during 1860–1920. Consequently, some of them became Fenians. American Fenianism was founded in 1859 as a militant Irish republican movement promoting the independence of Ireland from Great Britain. In 1859 the Indianapolis Circle of the Fenian Brotherhood was organized by Father Edward O'Flaherty, who recruited Fenian members throughout Indiana. The Fenians in Indianapolis were quiet during the Civil War until 1865 when a leadership dispute split the local brotherhood into two factions, one of which became defunct after a year. In 1866 the Fenians staged one of the largest meetings ever held in Indianapolis and subscribed a large amount of money on the occasion of a visit to Indianapolis by the Fenian president, who was engaged in a national publicity and fund-raising campaign for the brotherhood. American Fenians were most noted for organizing an army that made an unsuccessful invasion of Canada in the interest of Irish independence. In 1866, under the command of Captain James Haggerty, 130 armed Fenians went from Indianapolis to Buffalo, New York, where they joined a Fenian army. The invasion's failure left Indianapolis Fenians in disarray. But they reorganized and hosted a Fenian state convention in Indianapolis in 1868 when Indiana was divided into northern and southern Fenian districts. The renewal of internal dissension caused the Fenian organization to disband near the end of the decade. Subsequently, ex-Fenians in Indianapolis joined other Irish organizations. These included a military club called the Emmet Guards in honor of Robert Emmet (1778–1803), who was executed for his role in the Irish insurrection of 1803.[31]

Some of the Irish in Indiana participated in Irish nationalist movements in the 1880s. The Irish National Land League was founded in Ireland through the efforts of Michael Davitt (1846–1906), who was convinced that Irish nationalism required a pressing attack on the British landholding system in Ireland. Charles Stewart Parnell (1846–91), who was leader of the Irish Party in Parliament, was president of the Land League. The Irish National Land League was organized in the United States in 1880 to secure the moral and financial support of Irish Americans. Davitt informed the American press that the league, while seeking the abolition of landlordism, gave legal assistance and shelter to Irish tenants facing evictions. Subsequently, Irish Americans formed league branches in cities across the nation and donated hundreds of thousands of dollars to the league. The Indianapolis branch of the Irish National Land League was organized in 1881; it was active through 1886. The Irish National Land League Association of Indiana was also founded in 1881. The state association was headed by officers from Michigan City, Rushville, and Indianapolis in 1883. A further expression of Irish nationalism in the 1880s was the naming of Parnell Hall, which was a meeting place of Irish groups in Indianapolis.[32]

Irish nationalism also appeared in Indiana during World War I. Irish nationalists who had opposed British rule in Ireland were not eager to see the United States join Great Britain in the war in Europe. Thus, protests about American favoritism toward the Allies were made at joint German-Irish rallies staged in several Indiana cities in 1915. Similarly, Joseph Patrick O'Mahony's *Indiana Catholic* was the most important of the newspapers in the state taking the anti-British/pro-German editorial position. Nevertheless, many Irish Hoosiers fought and died in World War I.[33]

U-boat warfare on the Atlantic Ocean practically ended emigration from Ireland and from Europe generally for the duration of World War I. The mass emigration from Europe that preceded 1914 did not resume after the war, except for a brief moment. Consequently, the number of foreign-born Irish in the Indiana population fell in succeeding decades, and the Irish experience in Indiana changed much in the remainder of the twentieth century.

4. | Descendants of Immigrants and Irish Identity: *1920–2000*

THE TWENTIETH CENTURY IRISH EXPERIENCE IN INDIANA changed after the First World War. During the period 1920–2000 the Irish in Indiana were largely comprised of the descendants of immigrants who came from Ireland after 1815. The number of Irish natives in Indiana fell steadily from 7,271 in 1920 to 2,352 in 1950. During those years more than half of the Irish newcomers lived in Lake and Marion counties.[1]

Irish Catholics were concerned about the rise of the Ku Klux Klan in Indiana during the 1920s. Indiana had the highest ratio (92 percent) of native-born white population in the United States in 1920, and the Klan benefited from widespread nativism in the state. The Klan decried immigration as Indiana's total foreign-born population shrank from 159,663 in 1910 to 142,999 in 1930. The number of the state's foreign-born Irish declined sharply during the 1920s. In the main, Klan antiforeignism was directed at Indiana's immigrants from southern and eastern Europe, but its anti-Catholic venom spilled over on the Irish. William J. Mooney, the son of an Irish immigrant and a Catholic Democrat, related stories of Ku Klux Klan crosses burned on his porch in Indianapolis in the 1920s, according to his grandson William J. Mooney III. Dennis John O'Neill was among the Irish who criticized the Indiana Klan. In 1926, after graduating from Notre Dame,

TABLE C

NUMBER OF PERSONS BORN IN IRISH FREE STATE (PRIOR TO 1950) OR IN IRELAND (AFTER 1950) FOR TEN INDIANA COUNTIES WITH THE GREATEST IRISH FOREIGN-BORN POPULATIONS (GROUPED BY STATE REGIONS), 1930-2000*

Region and County	1930	1940	1950	1980	1990	2000
Northern						
Allen	160	97	103	44	31	42
Cass	78	44	—	—	—	—
Lake	720	474	517	144	122	41
La Porte	75	49	74	41	29	—
Porter	—	—	25	25	24	—
St. Joseph	286	198	183	55	71	47
Central						
Hamilton	—	—	—	—	39	70
Hendricks	—	—	—	—	—	41
Howard	54	—	—	—	—	—
Johnson	—	—	—	—	—	36
Madison	75	55	31	22	—	—
Marion	1,442	1,086	883	227	150	227
Putnam	—	—	—	—	—	39
Tippecanoe	87	44	—	48	24	—
Vigo	153	95	64	25	27	—
Wayne	—	—	27	—	—	—
Southern						
Bartholomew	—	—	—	—	—	37
Monroe	—	—	—	—	31	34
Vanderburgh	—	29	25	17	—	—

*Based on United States Department of Commerce, Bureau of the Census, *Census of Population* for the years 1930, 1940, 1950, 1980, 1990, 2000.

Headlines exposing Klan influence in and corruption of Indiana government, from the Pulitzer Prize-winning *Indianapolis Times*.

O'Neill was employed by the *Indianapolis Times,* covering state politics as a news reporter. O'Neill and editor Boyd Gurley started an investigation of Klan involvement in state politics. Their work led to a series of articles that exposed the Klan's corrupt political dealings and contributed to its decline in Indiana. In 1928 the *Times* was awarded a Pulitzer Prize for its Klan exposé.[2]

The Irish became less and less visible as an ethnic group in Indiana after 1920. Previously identifiable Irish neighborhoods disappeared as their residents dispersed. Meanwhile, the Irish left urban Catholic parishes where they had predominated. Also, fraternal and benevolent organizations with Irish names died out. Exoduses from old Irish areas in South Bend and Indianapolis were in progress during World War I, and Irish residential dispersals in these cities continued during the 1920s. In the 1930s former Irish neighborhoods in Fort Wayne, Madison, and New Albany remained as memories only, for example, of people interviewed by Federal Writers' Project researchers investigating the state's Irish history. As their residential patterns changed, the Irish often removed from one Catholic parish to another. Thus, the Irish were found in several Catholic parishes in some Indiana cities. By 1920 Irish Catholics in Terre Haute were attending St. Patrick, St. Ann, and St. Margaret churches as well as St. Joseph Church, which most of the Terre Haute Irish had attended at an earlier time. Mutual aid groups such as the Hibernian benevolent societies faded away before 1930 as did most of the Irish fraternal associations. The Ancient Order of Hibernians (AOH) survived in some Indiana cities after 1920, but its membership dwindled. For example, the AOH was active in Terre Haute until the end of the 1920s. Only AOH Division numbers 1 and 2 existed in Indianapolis in 1936, while in earlier times there had been six Hibernian units in that city.[3]

In consequence of these trends, studies covering Indiana history since World War I noted little activity of the Irish as an ethnic group. In their famous analysis of middle America, Robert and Helen Lynd hardly refer to the small Irish minority in Muncie. In the 1930s some Federal Writers' Project researchers concluded that the Irish in Indiana had been assimilated completely and had lost their distinctive ethnic identity. Irish immigrants had settled in the rural Madison Township of Dubois County in the nineteenth century. A Federal Writers' Project scholar who studied the history of Dubois County reported that the Irish of Madison Township had become amalgamated in the larger population and that the Irish group there had lost its national characteristics.[4] A Federal Writers' Project report on Indianapolis and Marion County stated, "The Irish made no effort to perpetuate their customs . . . and much of the transplanted culture of Erin has died out."[5]

Program cover of the 1950 Ancient Order of Hibernians St. Patrick's Day Celebration, the organization's 80th annual celebration.

Yet, paraphrasing Mark Twain, the report of the death of Irish ethnicity in Indiana was exaggerated. In some instances the Irish continued to act as an ethnic group, although they were less identifiable than in the past and less visible than groups of other nationalities. An Irish residential concentration remained from the 1920s to the 1940s in the neighborhood of St. Luke Church on Gary's east side. This reflected the fact that the number of Irish immigrants settling in Lake County increased through 1920. Indeed, Lake County received a large proportion of the state's Irish immigrants after 1920. Church congregations with sizable numbers of communicants of Irish ancestry could be found in Catholic parishes across Indiana in the 1930s and in the decades thereafter. For example, during the 1930s

Notre Dame University Archives, GBBY 4SG/228

Notre Dame football players, ca. 1920s.

Catholic families of Irish origin were still attending St. Mary Church near Floyd Knobs. This was the old Floyd County (Lafayette Township) church located in what nineteenth-century commentators called the Catholic Settlement on Little Indian Creek. Likewise, some Irish ethnic associations were founded in Indiana during the Depression decade and afterward. In 1936 the AOH had 527 members in Indianapolis. The AOH members there met bimonthly for entirely social and educational purposes. A St. Patrick's Day celebration on the Sunday preceding March 17 and a picnic on or near July 4 were annual events of the Indianapolis Hibernians. The Irish in Indiana remained connected with their ethnic heritage in a variety of individual and personal ways. Some remembered the immigration histories of their parents or grandparents. Undoubtedly, many Hoosiers with roots in Ireland identified with the Fighting Irish of Notre Dame, who became increasingly successful on the football fields after World War I. In the 1930s shamrock was growing on Patrick Flanigan's farm in the Bartholomew County "Sweet Ireland" Settlement, which had been started by Flanigan's immigrant father. Patrick Flanigan had visited Ireland and had brought back some of the shamrock. In the middle of the century, Martin Joseph Cleary owned the Fort Wayne Lincoln Life Baseball Team, which he publicized as the Shamrocks. Cleary's ancestors were Irish.[6]

Indianapolis Mayor Reginald H. Sullivan, 1931, with unnamed woman.

Indiana Historical Society, P 0130

The pace of socioeconomic progress among the Irish hastened in the twentieth century. After World War II the Irish advanced rapidly into the middle and upper-middle classes. Many children and grandchildren of Irish immigrants obtained the benefits of an academic education. In addition, others secured advanced training in professional schools and in graduate schools. Consequently, there were more professional and business people of Irish background during the latter twentieth century than in earlier times. They included lawyers and physicians, workers in insurance companies and banks, and professors and technicians. For example, William P. Flynn was an Indiana National Bank board chairman, and Andrew Sweeny was a State Life Insurance Company founder. In 1980 the occupational distribution of the Irish Catholics was similar to that of the urban Anglo-Saxon Protestants.[7]

The Irish in Indiana remained active in politics and government after 1920, retaining their ties to the Democratic Party. In 1928 William J. Mooney was state campaign director for Democratic presidential candidate Al Smith. Frank E. McKinney, an American Fletcher National Bank board chairman and a director of the Indiana Bell Telephone Company, was the Democratic Party national chairman during part of the Truman administration. As in the past, Irish politicians were elected to a variety of offices. Reginald H. Sullivan served as mayor of Indianapolis (1930–35, 1939–43). He was an Irish Protestant Democrat, as were a number of the mayors elected before him in that city. Al Feeney was the first Irish Catholic Democrat elected mayor of Indianapolis; he died in office in 1950. Later, John J. Barton was Indianapolis mayor. Another Irish Catholic Democrat, James H. Maguire, was mayor of Kokomo (1948–51).[8]

Many candidates of Irish ancestry were elected to the Indiana General Assembly in the twentieth century. At least 83 of the 1,258 assembly members were of Irish origin during 1930–70. In that period the Irish comprised 10 percent of the lawmakers (777) whose ancestry was known. Almost all of the Irish Catholic lawmakers of the period were Democrats. While only 5.2 percent of the assembly members were Catholic during 1891–1929, 14.1 percent of them were Catholic during 1931–69. Several Irish women won seats in the General Assembly during the 1960s. Anna Maloney, a retired teacher, represented Lake County in the House of Representatives (1961–72). During her career Maloney served as president of the Indiana Federation of Teachers and held memberships in several professional women's associations. In 1965 Katherine Margaret O'Connell Fruits and Cecilia M. Logan were elected to Marion County seats in the House. Fruits was a homemaker; Logan was an accountant. Both had been Democratic precinct committeewomen and leaders in county and state Democratic women's clubs.

Sheila Ann Johnston Klinker represented Tippecanoe County in the House (1983–84). Klinker, a teacher and an athletic coach, had been a Democratic state convention delegate and a worker in Democratic gubernatorial and congressional campaigns. All of the female Irish legislators were Democratic and Catholic. Fruits,

Sheila Klinker was first elected as an Indiana state representative in 1982. As of fall 2005 Klinker continued to represent the Lafayette and West Lafayette area (District 27) and served on the House Ways and Means Committee.

Indiana House of Representatives

Logan, and Klinker were representative of a growing number of Indiana families that were Irish on one side. Other state lawmakers with some Irish ancestry included Republican William Doyle Ruckelshaus, who became known nationally as deputy attorney general in the Nixon administration. Ruckelshaus was a Catholic of German and Irish origins. Similarly, Democratic state senator Frank Lewis O'Bannon of Corydon was a Methodist whose family lines were Irish, English, Dutch, German, and French. He served eighteen years in the state senate and two terms as Indiana lieutenant governor under Gov. Evan Bayh. Finally, O'Bannon was elected governor of Indiana in 1996 and re-elected in 2000.[9]

In the second half of the twentieth century most of the Irish in Indiana were generations removed from their immigrant forebears. The numbers of Irish immigrants in Indiana were only 825 in 1980, 733 in 1990, and 845 in 2000. Yet in 1990 almost a million Hoosiers claimed Irish ancestry. Irish Hoosiers increasingly married across nationality lines and sometimes outside the family's traditional faith. In consequence, family memories of Ireland grew dimmer. The Irish ethnic group became less visible and less conscious of itself than it had been in the 1930s. At the same time, the relatively few Irish immigrants of the recent period remembered well the Emerald Isle. Noreen Hall of county Cork emigrated in 1949 and located in Highland (Lake County). In 1984 she still remembered that her Christmases in Ireland "were beautiful, and holy." Mary Jones of county Mayo also settled in Highland after departing Ireland in 1955. She fondly recalled Irish folk dancing, which she taught in Indiana for sixteen years.[10]

A great many Irish Hoosiers born outside the immigrant generation remained tied to their Irish family histories in various ways. A 1978 account of the Irish in Indianapolis stated: "Capt. [David T.] Shea wears the 1889 fireman's badge issued his grandfather, Jeremiah, who came from County Kerry. His brothers, Joseph and James, also are fire captains, and three other brothers . . . are firemen."[11] Similarly, the historic devotion of the Irish family to the Catholic Church was seen in the life of Edward T. O'Meara, whose parents were emigrants from county Tipperary. O'Meara was archbishop of the Archdiocese of Indianapolis (1980–92).[12]

There were many Irish societies in Indiana in 1900 when immigrants still made up a large part of the state's Irish community. One hundred years later it was less usual for Irish Hoosiers to organize along ethnic lines, but in some places there were associations rooted in Irish organizational history. Established in 1959 in Lake County, the Friendly Sons of Erin was still active in the 1980s when it gave Shamrock awards and John F. Kennedy awards for public service. The venerable AOH was alive and well in Indianapolis and South Bend in the year 2000. Founded in 1958, Indianapolis AOH Division #3 maintained continuous existence and active programs through 2000. AOH members, as in the past, were required to be practicing Catholics of Irish ancestry. A local officer reported in 1992 that the AOH had more than three hundred members in Indianapolis. Division #3 regularly celebrated St. Patrick's Day. In addition, it held social affairs such as dances and Irish-day picnics and charity events, including raffles. This AOH division made many donations over the course of its existence to various public and private charities and Catholic Action programs. It also supported a University of Notre Dame scholarship for a student of Irish ancestry. In the electronic age of communication, the AOH in Indianapolis offered an Internet Web site including links to live news from Ireland. South Bend's James McDivitt Division of the AOH, established in 1965, still was holding monthly meetings in 2000 and staging special events such as a St. Patrick's Day dinner, according to its current treasurer.[13]

A revitalization of organized Irish American activities in Indiana during the latter decades of the twentieth century owed something to a larger ethnic phenomenon occurring in the United States at the time. Late in the 1960s, ethnicity began to rise in prominence in American society, culture, and politics. This followed several decades that had seen a decline in organized activities by the Irish and other European ethnic groups in the United States. Mass emigration from Europe had ended during World War I and had not resumed thereafter. Consequently, the number of foreign-born Europeans in the country had fallen from the 1930s through the 1960s, eventually becoming a very small proportion of the nation's population. This was accompanied by a lowering of ethnic consciousness in the nation.

Ethnic historians Leonard Dinnerstein and David M. Reimers show that multiple factors underlay the resurgence of ethnic awareness and activities in the late 1960s. Perhaps the catalyst among them was the combination of the Civil Rights and the Black Nationalist movements in the 1960s that together made the nation aware of the African American group's presence in the United States and its ethnic heritage in Africa and in America. Soon other groups, including Native Americans, Mexican Americans, and Italian Americans, launched similar movements emphasizing rights and ethnic heritages. By the early 1970s the revival of ethnic activism across the country engendered the establishment of new ethnic organizations, influenced cities to proclaim special ethnic heritage days, and prompted universities to initiate ethnic programs, such as African American studies and Jewish studies. The Keough Institute for Irish Studies at the University of Notre Dame was established in 1993 as a result of this movement.[14]

At this time there was an outpouring of new books about the Irish and many other ethnic groups in the United States. (See the "Selected Bibliography" in this volume for Irish examples.) Late in the 1970s "the *Roots* phenomenon" contributed to a nationwide awareness of family history, a cornerstone of ethnic consciousness. The weeklong television miniseries *Roots* followed the story of an African American family from its origin in Africa through its slavery experiences. Record audiences viewed it in January 1977, and, subsequently, genealogy became extraordinarily popular throughout the country. Vast numbers of Americans of all colors and ethnicities did family history research. Twenty years later a wide spectrum of Americans was inspired by dazzling performances of Irish step dancers when *Riverdance* and *Lord of the Dance* were aired by television's Public Broadcasting System (PBS). Also, in the 1990s National Public Radio affiliates in Indiana and elsewhere regularly broadcast the *Thistle and Shamrock*, a popular program of traditional and modern music of Ireland and Scotland.[15]

The renewed interest in things ethnic that followed the 1960s was seen in Indiana, and the Indiana Historical Society's publication of *Peopling Indiana: The Ethnic Experience* (1996) was evidence

Indianapolis Irish Festival

Celtic Footforce performs at the 2004 Indianapolis Irish Festival, an annual event that celebrates Irish culture and heritage.

that it was still alive as the century closed.[16] New Irish organizations and activities were initiated in Indiana in this post-1960s atmosphere. They were largely devoted to preservation and celebration of the Irish cultural and social heritage, often combined with acts of charity. In some Indiana cities, locally popular "Irish pubs," often established after 1970, raised the Irish profile.

This resurgence of Irish identity and community life in Indiana was seen, for instance, in Terre Haute, Indianapolis, and South Bend. Starting in 1983, an annual St. Patrick's Day parade and party were held in Terre Haute the weekend prior to March 17. Meantime, it became the custom for the city to name someone of Irish ancestry as Honorary Mayor of Terre Haute on St. Patrick's Day.

The founders of these celebrations were mainly from local families of Irish descent, such as the Bolins and the Cahills, but some were natives of Ireland. Joe and Jeanne Donnelly helped plan the first St. Patrick's Day Dinner and Dance in Terre Haute's St. Patrick School. The Donnellys, who were raised and trained in the culinary arts in Dublin, stayed in touch with their Irish families and friends, making biennial trips to Dublin. In 1992 some seven hundred tickets were sold for the tenth annual St. Patrick's Day affair in Terre Haute, and about half of those attending were of Irish ancestry. In the 1980s and 1990s Terre Haute's Irish pubs also marked St. Patrick's Day. Reilly's Tavern on North Third Street and the Sonka Irish Pub on Wabash Avenue offered Irish food and drink on the holiday. Sonka's was an old tavern with a Romanian name, but its several owners were of Irish descent starting in the early 1970s. Interest in the formal study of Irish American history grew in this new age of ethnic consciousness. History graduate students at Indiana State University did research on Irish themes. For example, in 1986 Sharon Bryant Hinkle, whose ancestors were Irish, completed a master's thesis about Irish immigrants in Terre Haute on the eve of the Civil War. Trevor Gordon, who was born and reared in Northern Ireland, completed a master's thesis in 2001 on the nineteenth-century Irish National Land League's activities in Indiana.[17]

After the 1960s Irish American life in Indianapolis was enriched with the appearance of new Irish organizations and activities. The Irish Step Dancers of Indianapolis were founded around 1977 according to Pat Spellacy, one of the group's organizers. Most of the dancers were young females of Irish ancestry. A variety of teachers over the years taught them traditional Irish dances. One teacher, who had been a former national dance champion in Ireland, commuted from Chicago to Indianapolis. The dancers, who participated in dance contests and gave exhibitions, were still active early in the twenty-first century. The Irish American Heritage Society was founded in Indianapolis in 1980 and remained vital in the next decade. In the 1990s, according to society officer Juanita Taylor, it engaged in educational, cultural, and musical activities. A society newsletter kept members informed, and the organization staffed cultural and merchandise booths at Indianapolis's annual international festival. The society held monthly meetings with programs that featured Irish history, culture, myths, presidents, and holidays. Not possessing its own hall, the organization held its meetings in various Knights of Columbus facilities and at the Dooley O'Toole Restaurant. The society maintained outreach activities in Indianapolis schools where programs on Ireland were presented, provided speakers for senior citizens groups, and sponsored traditional Irish musical events with entertainers such as Roby O'Connell. The Irish American Heritage Society participated in Indianapolis's annual St. Patrick's Day parade and also celebrated the day with a dinner and program of Irish music and poetry.[18]

The 1990s witnessed more new efforts to grow organized Irish life in the Indianapolis area. Hibernian women's activities were restored. St. Bridget's Division of the Ladies Ancient Order of Hibernians (LAOH) had existed in Indianapolis for a time after 1950 before eventually becoming defunct. Then in 1995 Irish women founded the Our Lady of Knock Division of the LAOH, and it was still active in Indianapolis ten years later. In addition to being practicing Catholics, members were required to be Irish by birth, ancestry, or adoption or to be the mother or wife of a Hibernian. Identifying itself as a Catholic Action group, the LAOH held monthly meetings and supported a variety of charities, including a food pantry, foreign missions, and social welfare work among women and Native Americans. These Hibernian women, for example, made contributions to causes aimed at protecting women from domestic abuse and to programs offering material assistance to needy young mothers to enable them to support their infants.[19]

Also in 1995, the Indianapolis Firefighters Emerald Society Pipes and Drums Corps was formed following a firefighter's funeral. Its members, all firefighters, devoted themselves to a Celtic music

Dan Davis, Indianapolis Firefighters Emerald Society Pipes and Drums

Members of the Indianapolis Firefighters Emerald Society Pipes and Drums stand outside the Indiana State House, 2005.

tradition with Irish and Scottish roots. They built a repertoire of Irish and Scottish tunes from "Danny Boy" to "Blue Bells of Scotland" and performed at a variety of local public venues, most notably at St. Patrick's Day events, Indianapolis Irish Festival, and Burns Suppers. Emerald Societies associated with police and fire departments had existed for decades in cities across the nation. Typically, they had been formed to foster the tradition of public service performed by Irish police officers and firefighters. The Indiana Emerald Society established in Evansville, for example, became a chapter of the National Conference of Law Enforcement Emerald Societies in 1999. It called attention to Irish culture, and its pipe band performed at police, fire, and military funerals.[20]

The Indiana Irish Cultural Society was formed in 1996 and held general meetings on themes such as Irish literature, music, and genealogy. In 2002 it promoted a local appearance of Northern Ireland-born Seamus Deane, a poet, novelist, and professor of Irish Studies at the University of Notre Dame. The Indiana Irish Cultural Society also sponsored the Indianapolis Annual Feis and in 2002 saw its fifth annual Irish dance competition conducted in the city.[21]

The Indianapolis Irish Festival was first staged in 1995, reflecting the rising popularity at the time of public activities associated with the Irish. A few local people of Irish descent, including Alice Field Davis, conceived the Festival. They wished to make Irish culture more available to the public and to call attention to the positive roles of Irish folk in Indiana. The initial Indianapolis Irish Festival at the State Fairgrounds drew about five thousand people, proving to be financially viable. The Claddagh Irish Pub became its principal sponsor. Eventually, more than two dozen additional backers, including a wide range of commercial enterprises and public institutions, provided contributions and support. Attendance grew to about twenty thousand by 2004 when the Festival was held in Military Park at White River State Park in Indianapolis. The tenth annual Indy Irish Fest was a three-day weekend affair in September celebrating Irish heritage. Some of its Sunday events were headlined as Celtic Mass, Full Irish Breakfast, Celtic Canines, Parade of the Clans, and Sheep Herding Exhibitions. The Festival raised funds that were donated to Indianapolis charities and community organizations. Festival promoters declared that in 2003 ten thousand dollars was given to Irish organizations and students engaged in Irish cultural studies. Organizations benefiting from Festival funds were the AOH, LAOH, Irish Children's Fund, Indiana Irish Cultural Society, Irish Step Dancers of Indianapolis, Indianapolis Firefighters Emerald Society, and Indianapolis Annual Feis.[22]

Indy Irish Fest's chief sponsor, the Claddagh Irish Pub, was one of a variety of Irish pubs that existed in the Indianapolis vicinity at different times in the late twentieth century and after. Some of their owners had Irish backgrounds while others did not; some of these taverns were considerably newer than others. The patrons of some were largely persons of Irish descent while others catered to the general public. All these pubs featured Irish themes and raised local consciousness of Irish identity, and some also provided settings for local Irish social and cultural life. Among them were the Dooley O'Toole Restaurant and Muldoon's Pub in the Carmel vicinity and Golden Ace Inn and Griffin's County Kerry Pub in Indianapolis. The Golden Ace Inn, at the turn of the latest century, was an example of a pub serving as a social gathering place for the local Irish and a forum for sessions of live music in the Irish tradition. It was in an older neighborhood off the commercial track for the general public but known to many Irish folk thirsty for Irish drink, literary expressions, and live music.[23]

As elsewhere, Irish self-consciousness and Irish cultural activities grew in South Bend after the 1960s, especially near the century's end. Perhaps the most notable example of this came with the founding of the Shamrock Club in September 1993. Under the leadership of local health care services executive Michael P. Devine, it was established as a not-for-profit cultural organization "for Irish only." The Shamrock Club launched its first St. Patrick's Day celebration in 1994 with events promising "plenty of music, food, blarney and blather." These festivities featured the Makem Brothers and Brian Sullivan, a local group that had been performing traditional Irish music for about three years. The Shamrock Club in 1997 inaugurated its first St. Patrick's Day Parade starting at East Jefferson Street and Frances Street in downtown South Bend. Hundreds watched the 1998 parade on a cold and windy day. Attendance at the following celebration at the Century Center exceeded expectations, requiring many additional tables. After the parade in 1999, more than a thousand people came to the Century Center St. Patrick's Day affair organized by the Shamrock Club.[24]

In the twenty-first century, the club extended membership to those who "love all things Irish/Celtic." Alan A. Bigger was Shamrock Club president in 2005. He was born in Belfast and raised in Dublin. The organization still sponsored the annual parade and other events including Half Way to St. Pat's Day parties held in September. Meanwhile, it sometimes joined in common efforts with the South Bend Division of the AOH, which held fund-raisers for charitable causes. The Shamrock Club's Web page publicized many other Irish/Celtic activities then occurring in South Bend.[25]

The popularity of traditional Irish music and dance in this later age also grew in the South Bend vicinity. Young performers perfected their arts and found venues to express them in St. Joseph County. Kennedy's Kitchen was formed in 1998 and became one of the South Bend area's most successful groups performing traditional Irish instrumental and vocal music, including dance tunes and pub songs. Often performing with Kennedy's Kitchen was the Celtic Fire Dance Company. This was a new group of South Bend area young women highly trained in step dancing. Established in 2002, the Fiddler's Hearth Public House in South Bend shortly became a setting for Irish music, dance, poetry, and storytelling. Operated by the Meehan family, it aspired to be a gathering place for Celtic artists and the general public. The Hearth offered Irish/Celtic food and drinks and a weekly calendar of live entertainment; for example, Monday evenings were devoted to an "Open Irish Music Session." Also, early in the new century, the popularity of Irish culture in South Bend undoubtedly induced local WSND-FM Radio to air a weekly Celtic music program called *Celtic Traditions*. This interest in Irish culture and in Ireland was noticeable in the business market. Cragan's Irish Import Shop was commercially viable in South Bend during the 1990s. The Fighting Irish of the University of Notre Dame remained a prime factor in maintaining Irish identity in South Bend, but the post 1960s ethnic phenomena raised Irish awareness to a new level there as elsewhere by the year 2000.[26]

The renewal of Irish identity was uneven across Indiana in the late twentieth century, but at least once a year the Irish in the state comprised a community that was conscious of itself and visible to others. St. Patrick's Day was celebrated in large and small cities in Indiana in the year 2000. The Irish of Terre Haute gathered at St. Patrick Church for a parade starting at the intersection of 19th and Poplar streets, which, as usual, was entirely painted with a green shamrock on a field of white.[27] On March 17 the descendants of Erin in Indiana, as those elsewhere, were happy to be Irish, and everyone else was welcome to be Irish.

Conclusion

T HE PRECEDING PAGES OFFER ONLY A GLIMPSE OF PAST
Irish life in Indiana. Deeper perceptions must
await the publication of scholarly articles and monographs focusing on narrowly defined aspects of the
Irish experience there. Such works on the Irish in
Indiana are rare, leaving almost an open field for
future scholarship. Mentioned here are a few of the
innumerable neglected Irish themes in Indiana's
past. Primary research is needed, for example, on the
early stages of urban Irish ethnic community development for the period 1830–70 in such cities as Fort
Wayne, Indianapolis, Lafayette, and Terre Haute
that saw the Irish foreign-born population signifi-
cantly increase throughout these decades. Also lacking is original research for the years 1870–1914 that
witnessed the growth and coming of age of Irish ethnic communities in various Indiana cities amidst a
gradual decline in the numbers of newcomers from
Ireland. Original studies of the nineteenth-century
Irish in Indiana's small cities, towns, and rural counties are needed as well. The urban and rural experiences of the Irish in Indiana had economic, social,
cultural, and political dimensions that scholars can
explore.

Specialized studies of the Irish in Indiana can
comment on the many issues in the generations-
long scholarly dialogue about immigration and
ethnicity in United States history. Issues of greatest interest in this scholarly discussion changed

over the twentieth century. Early scholarship, often by sociologists, described nineteenth-century immigrants as powerless victims of great forces and of urban industrial pathologies that exposed them to deteriorating social settings plagued by crime, disease, and pauperism. After the 1960s, scholars, including historians, redirected the discussion to less negative factors, while not denying that problems existed in nineteenth-century immigrant slum districts. These scholars gave evidence that urban immigrants were not passive then, showing that they played active roles in cities, taking the lead in forming nationality communities composed of a variety of ethnic institutions and organizations. (See David Ward's historiographical commentary on changing scholarly perspectives regarding urban ghettos and slums.)[1]

Kevin Kenny's new volume describes a comparable transformation since the 1960s in the written discussion about the Irish American past. Recent books, journal articles, and a doctoral dissertation about Irish Americans discuss historical memory, gender, race, and issues of socioeconomic class, such as organized labor. These newer studies in Irish American history tend to be interdisciplinary in nature. Among other new perceptions is one interpreting the movement out of Ireland, not as emigration, but as an aspect of an international migration in an Atlantic World. This makes the story of the sending country as important as that of the receiving one.[2]

Institutional libraries and archives possess enough primary source materials on the Irish in Indiana to support some basic scholarly research in this area. These holdings include United States census records, city directories, local newspapers, citizenship naturalization records, transcripts of oral interviews, and manuscripts. For example, original manuscripts of the Indiana Federal Writers' Project/Program are housed at Indiana State University's Cunningham Memorial Library. The researchers of this New Deal era work project collected information about the Irish in the 1930s as well as about many other aspects of Indiana life and history.

How can a researcher use materials held by such libraries and archives, for example, census records, to comment on a dimension of Irish history in Indiana, such as gender issues? The public has access to manuscript population schedules (microfilm) recorded in each census through 1930. These schedules list information about each person counted in a household. They reveal the head of household. Censuses from 1850 onward give a person's country or state of birth, gender, age, occupation, and other such facts. The general characteristics of Irish-born women in an Indiana city, say Lafayette in 1850, can be derived from its population schedules. Irish-born women and men can be identified and counted. Then the proportion of women and men in Lafayette's 1850 Irish population can be calculated. Similarly, the average ages of Irish women and men in the city can be determined.

Likewise, this approach can show the proportion of Irish-born women who were listed as head of household. It can reveal the percentage of Irish immigrant women counted as living single in a household where no one else with her surname was present—for example, a boarding house with female occupants only. The most typical Irish immigrant family form in the city can be found in this way. These schedules list some households containing children living with an adult female and an adult male all having the same surname. Also recorded are households accommodating three generations with the same family name and other households carrying two or more surnames. The occupations listed in the schedules can be used to distinguish middle-class and working-class Irish-born women and to determine a class's proportional size. Such findings for a city in two or more census years can be compared to discover whether the profile of the Irish-born women changed over time. Likewise, comparisons of such findings for cities inside and outside Indiana can be valuable in advancing the dialogue about Irish American history.

Those researching most Irish themes in Indiana cannot rely entirely on materials found at present in the kinds of institutions already mentioned here. Researchers must take the initiative in seeking out additional sources. These may be found, for example, in the membership, marriage, birth, and death records of Catholic parishes in Indiana. Researchers can contact descendants of Irish immigrants who have knowledge of surviving written or oral sources. Undoubtedly, Irish folk today have kept some of the correspondence of their Irish-born ancestors. The papers of local Irish organizations and institutions in Indiana may well exist outside of library collections. Descendants of Ireland can assist in the building of Irish American history by bringing the existence of these kinds of sources to the attention of research institutions.

Notes

INTRODUCTION

1. David J. Bodenhamer and Robert G. Barrows, eds., with the assistance of David G. Vanderstel, *Encyclopedia of Indianapolis* (Bloomington: Indiana University Press, 1994), 827–29; Robert M. Taylor Jr. and Connie A. McBirney, eds., *Peopling Indiana: The Ethnic Experience* (Indianapolis: Indiana Historical Society, 1996), 244–73.

2. David M. Emmons, *The Butte Irish: Class and Ethnicity in an American Mining Town, 1875–1925* (Urbana: University of Illinois Press, 1989); David T. Gleeson, *The Irish in the South, 1815–1877* (Chapel Hill: University of North Carolina Press, 2001); Cheryl T. Herr, *Critical Regionalism and Cultural Studies: From Ireland to the American Midwest* (Gainesville: University Press of Florida, 1996); David G. Holmes, *Irish in Wisconsin* (Madison: Wisconsin Historical Society Press, 2004); Ann Regan, *Irish in Minnesota* (St. Paul: Minnesota Historical Society Press, 2002). Also, see Dermot Quinn, *The Irish in New Jersey: Four Centuries of American Life* (New Brunswick: Rutgers University Press, 2004).

CHAPTER 1. COLONISTS AND SETTLERS: 1740–1832

1. Maldwyn A. Jones, *American Immigration* (Chicago: University of Chicago Press, 1974), 22; John D. Barnhart and Dorothy L. Riker, *Indiana to 1816: The Colonial Period* (Indianapolis: Indiana Historical Bureau and Indiana Historical Society, 1971), 71–93.

2. Albert T. Volwiler, *George Croghan and the Westward Movement, 1741–1782* (Cleveland: Arthur Clark, 1926), 21–23, 36; Nicholas B. Wainwright, *George Croghan: Wilderness Diplomat* (Chapel Hill: University of North Carolina Press, 1959), 3, 14–15; Barnhart and Riker, *Indiana to 1816*, 98, 105; Eugene H. Roseboom and Francis P. Weisenburger, *A History of Ohio* (Columbus: Ohio State Archaeological and Historical Society, 1961), 20.

3. Wainwright, *George Croghan*, 4.

4. Ibid., 16–21, 38; Barnhart and Riker, *Indiana to 1816*, 123, 124, 125–26, 152–55; John D. Barnhart and Donald F. Carmony, *Indiana: From*

Frontier to Industrial Commonwealth (New York: Lewis Publishing, 1954), 1:49; Roseboom and Weisenburger, *History of Ohio*, 27–28.

5. Barnhart and Carmony, *Indiana*, 1:77–79, 98–99; Leonard C. Helderman, "Northwest Expedition of George Rogers Clark," *Mississippi Valley Historical Review* 25 (December 1938): 317–24; Jones, *American Immigration*, 22, 108.

6. Rebecca A. Shepherd et al., eds., *A Biographical Directory of the Indiana General Assembly, 1816–1899* (Indianapolis: Indiana Historical Bureau, 1980), 1:319.

7. Barnhart and Carmony, *Indiana*, 1:152.

8. Archibald Shaw, ed., *History of Dearborn County, Indiana, Her People, Industries and Institutions* (Indianapolis: B. F. Bowen and Co., 1915), 148–49.

9. *Atlas of Dearborn County, Indiana* (Philadelphia: Lake, Griffing and Stevenson, 1875), 18.

10. Barnhart and Carmony, *Indiana*, 1:151.

11. Jones, *American Immigration*, 92–97, 108–10, 117–18.

12. Harlow Lindley, ed., *Indiana As Seen By Early Travelers, Indiana Historical Collections* (Indianapolis: Indiana Historical Commission, 1916), 3:463, 473.

13. Ibid., 524.

14. Thomas T. McAvoy, *The Catholic Church in Indiana, 1789–1834* (New York: Columbia University Press, 1940), 16–20, 169; Herman J. Alerding, *A History of the Catholic Church in the Diocese of Vincennes* (Indianapolis: Carlon and Hollenbeck, 1883), 29, 81, 379–80; Charles Blanchard, ed., *History of the Catholic Church in Indiana* (Logansport, IN: A. W. Bowen and Co., 1898), 1:251–52; J. Lawrence Richardt, "A Narrative History of Saint Joseph Church, Terre Haute, Indiana, 1838–1872" (master's thesis, Indiana State University, 1969), 6–7, 9; Shaw, *History of Dearborn County*, 404.

15. *History of the Ohio Falls Cities and Their Counties* (Cleveland: L. A. Williams and Co., 1882), 2:302, 309–10, 314; Alerding, *Diocese of Vincennes*, 341–42.

16. Elfrieda Lang, "Irishmen in Northern Indiana before 1850," *Mid-America: An Historical Review*, 36 (1954): 190–91.

CHAPTER 2. NEWCOMERS IN AN AGE OF MASS IMMIGRATION: 1832–1860

1. "Cash for Canal Hands," *Indianapolis, Indiana Journal*, August 1832, quoted in Charles R. Poinsatte, *Fort Wayne during the Canal Era, 1828–1855: A Study of a Western Community in the Middle Period of American History, Indiana Historical Collections* (Indianapolis: Indiana Historical Bureau, 1969), 46:59.

2. J. Lawrence Richardt, "A Narrative History of St. Joseph Church, Terre Haute, Indiana, 1838–1872" (master's thesis, Indiana State University, 1969) 31; Poinsatte, *Fort Wayne during the Canal Era*, 46:60–61.

3. Maldwyn A. Jones, *American Immigration* (Chicago: University of Chicago Press, 1974), 130–31.

4. *Fort Wayne Sentinel*, August 27, 1842, quoted in Poinsatte, *Fort Wayne during the Canal Era*, 46:60.

5. Jones, *American Immigration*, 131; Poinsatte, *Fort Wayne during the Canal Era*, 46:60–61.

6. Richardt, "History of St. Joseph Church," 31; Alvin A. Harlow, *Old Towpaths: The Story of the American Canal Era* (New York: D. Appleton and Co., 1926), 267; Poinsatte, *Fort Wayne during the Canal Era*, 46:63, 144; John D. Barnhart and Donald F. Carmony, *Indiana: From Frontier to Industrial Commonwealth* (New York: Lewis Publishing, 1954) 1:418.

7. Paul Fatout, *Indiana Canals* (West Lafayette, IN: Purdue University Studies, 1972), 85.

8. *History of Allen County, Indiana* (Chicago: Kingman Brothers, 1880), 93.

9. Father Stephen Badin, quoted in William McNamara, *The Catholic Church on the Northern Indiana Frontier, 1789–1844* (Washington, DC: Catholic University of America, 1931), 61.

10. Richardt, "History of Saint Joseph Church," 31.

11. Fatout, *Indiana Canals*, 58; Poinsatte, *Fort Wayne during the Canal Era*, 46:62.

12. McNamara, *Catholic Church on the Northern Indiana Frontier*, 61.

13. Fatout, *Indiana Canals*, 85.

14. Emma Lou Thornbrough, *Indiana in the Civil War Era, 1850–1880* (Indianapolis: Indiana Historical Bureau and Indiana Historical Society, 1965), 634.

15. John H. O'Donnell, "The Catholic Church in Northern Indiana: 1830–1857," *The Catholic Historical Review* 25 (July 1939): 140.

16. Canal contracts quoted in Poinsatte, *Fort Wayne during the Canal Era*, 46:61.

17. Ibid., 61–62.

18. McNamara, *Catholic Church on the Northern Indiana Frontier*, 61.

19. Richardt, "History of St. Joseph Church," 42.

20. Fatout, *Indiana Canals*, 59.

21. Mary Salesia Godecker, *Simon Bruté de Remur, First Bishop of Vincennes* (St. Meinrad, IN: St. Meinrad Historical Essays, 1931), 361–62; Harlow, *Old Towpaths*, 236–37, 267; Barnhart and Carmony, *Indiana*, 2:447; Elfrieda Lang, "Irishmen in Northern Indiana before 1850," *Mid-America: An Historical Review*, 36 (1954): 191–92; Fatout, *Indiana Canals*, 58, 69; Poinsatte, *Fort Wayne during the Canal Era*, 46:62–63; Willis Richardson, "History of the Wabash and Erie Canal" (master's thesis, Indiana University, 1925), 77–78; *Indianapolis, Indiana Journal*, July 31, 1835; David Burr to Gov. Noah Noble, December 30, 1835, *Indiana Documentary Journal, 1835*, House Report no. 18, 1–4.

22. *Indiana Documentary Journal, 1835*, 2.

23. Ibid.

24. Ibid.

25. Ibid.

26. *Fort Wayne Sentinel* quoted in *Indianapolis, Indiana Journal*, July 31, 1835.

27. *Indiana Documentary Journal, 1835*, 2–3.

28. Godecker, *Simon Bruté de Remur*, 345.

29. *Indiana Documentary Journal, 1835*, 3.

30. Ibid.

31. *Indiana House Journal, 1835–1836*, 26.

32. *Indiana Documentary Journal, 1835*, 3; Barnhart and Carmony, *Indiana*, 2:447; Godecker, *Simon Bruté de Remur*, 361–62.

33. Richardt, "History of Saint Joseph Church," 7; Edward A. Leary, *Indianapolis: The Story of a City* (Indianapolis: Bobbs-Merrill, 1971), 35; Barnhart and Carmony, *Indiana*, 2:447.

34. Herman J. Alerding, *A History of the Catholic Church in the Diocese of Vincennes* (Indianapolis: Carlon and Hollenbeck, 1883), 29; Charles Blanchard, ed., *History of the Catholic Church in Indiana* (Logansport, IN: A. W. Bowen and Co., 1898), 1:51; O'Donnell, "Catholic Church in Northern Indiana," 141; McNamara, *Catholic Church on the Northern Indiana Frontier*, 61–62; Richardt, "History of St. Joseph Church," 42.

35. Poinsatte, *Fort Wayne during the Canal Era*, 46:141–48; Herman J. Alerding, *The Diocese of Fort Wayne, 1857– September 22, 1907: A Book of Historical Reference, 1669–1907* (Fort Wayne, IN: Archer Printing, 1907), 203.

36. McNamara, *Catholic Church on the Northern Indiana Frontier*, 62; Thomas B. Helm, ed., *History of Cass County, Indiana* (Chicago: Brant and Fuller, 1886), 435–36; Jehu Z. Powell, *History of Cass County, Indiana* (Chicago: Lewis Publishing, 1913), 1: 435–36; Alerding, *Diocese of Fort Wayne*, 208–10, 211–12, 213–14.

37. *Biographical Record and Portrait Album of Tippecanoe County, Indiana* (Chicago: Lewis Publishing, 1888), 284–85.

38. Ibid.; Alerding, *Diocese of Fort Wayne*, 217–18.

39. Alerding, *Diocese of Vincennes*, 421–25, 469–70; Andrew W. Young, *History of Wayne County, Indiana: From Its First Settlement to the Present Time* (Cincinnati: Robert Clarke and Co., 1872), 407; *History of Wayne County, Indiana* (Chicago: Inter-State Publishing, 1884), 2:150–51; William R. Holloway, *Indianapolis: A Historical and Statistical Sketch of the Railroad City* (Indianapolis: Indianapolis Journal Print, 1870), 239; B. R. Sulgrove, *History of Indianapolis and Marion County, Indiana* (Philadelphia: L. H. Everts and Co., 1884), 406.

40. Alerding, *Diocese of Vincennes*, 452–57; Richardt, "History of Saint Joseph Church," 18–30.

41. Parishioner quoted in Richardt, "History of Saint Joseph Church," 41.

42. *History of the Ohio Falls Cities and Their Counties* (Cleveland: L. A. Williams and Co., 1882), 2:209–10, 310, 314–15; Archibald Shaw, ed.,

History of Dearborn County, Indiana, Her People, Industries and Institutions (Indianapolis: B. F. Bowen and Co., 1915), 404–05; Alerding, *Diocese of Vincennes*, 333–34, 341–42, 379–80.

43. Gil R. Stormont, *History of Gibson County, Indiana* (Indianapolis: B. F. Bowen and Co., 1914), 98.

44. Fatout, *Indiana Canals*, 141.

45. Stormont, *History of Gibson County*, 99.

46. O'Donnell, "Catholic Church in Northern Indiana," 137–38, 143; Donald T. Zimmer, "Madison, Indiana, 1811–1860: A Study in the Process of City Building" (PhD diss., Indiana University, 1974), 61; Jefferson Co.-261.4-Irish, microfilm, roll 11, frame 1157, Marion Co.-260.5-Ethnology, microfilm, roll 16, frame 0798, Indiana Federal Writers' Project/Program collection, Indiana State University Library, Terre Haute, Indiana (hereafter cited as IFWPP); John Aylward, "Immigrant Settlement Patterns in South Bend, 1865–1917" (typescript, Northern Indiana Historical Society, 1971), 4–5; Barnhart and Carmony, *Indiana*, 2:38; Richardt, "History of Saint Joseph Church," 43; Charles E. Robert, *Evansville: Her Commerce and Manufactures* (Evansville: Courier, 1874), 532.

47. Percentages computed by author. See Table A, p. 38.

48. See Table B, p. 41; Gregory S. Rose, "The Distribution of Indiana's Ethnic and Racial Minorities in 1850" (typescript, Ethnic History Project, Indiana Historical Society, 1989), 16–17.

49. Poinsatte, *Fort Wayne during the Canal Era*, 46:60; Elbert J. Benton, "The Wabash Trade Route in the Development of the Old Northwest," *Johns Hopkins University Studies in Historical and Political Science* 21 (January-February 1903): 97–98; McNamara, *"Catholic Church on the Northern Indiana Frontier,"* 62; "1850 Census Foreign-Born for Indiana" (unpublished manuscript, Education Division, Indiana Historical Society, 1991), 6; "1860 Census Foreign-Born for Indiana" (unpublished manuscript, Education Division, Indiana Historical Society, 1991), 7; see Table B, p. 41.

50. Lang, "Irishmen in Northern Indiana," 193; Barnhart and Carmony, *Indiana*, 2:14.

51. Computations by author. Figures obtained from the nationality by township section of "1860 Census Foreign-Born for Indiana," 14–63.

52. Jones, *American Immigration*, 130; Dean R. Esslinger, *Immigrants and the City: Ethnicity and Mobility in a Nineteenth-Century Midwestern Community* (Port Washington, NY: Kennikat Press, 1975), 87–88, 94; Sharon B. Hinkle, "Irish Immigrants in Terre Haute, Indiana, in 1860: A Comparative Study" (master's thesis, Indiana State University, 1987), 10, 20, 22; Lang, "Irishmen in Northern Indiana," 192–93, 195–96; Thornbrough, *Indiana in the Civil War*, 552; Poinsatte, *Fort Wayne during the Canal Era*, 46:65.

53. Jones, *American Immigration*, 132–34; Lang, "Irishmen in Northern Indiana," 197; Thornbrough, *Indiana in the Civil War*, 552.

54. "1850 Census Foreign-Born for Indiana," 37; Hinkle, "Irish Immigrants in Terre Haute," 41, 59, 61; Zimmer, "Madison, Indiana," 59, 62, 72; Esslinger, *Immigrants and the City*, 52–54; Aylward, "Immigrant Settlement Patterns in South Bend," 4–5.

55. Poinsatte, *Fort Wayne during the Canal Era*, 46:148; Robert, *Evansville: Her Commerce and Manufactures*, 534; *Album of Tippecanoe County*, 289; *Ohio Falls Cities*, 2:210; Alerding, *Diocese of Vincennes*, 334, 373–74, 428; Sulgrove, *History of Indianapolis*, 407; Alerding, *Diocese of Fort Wayne*, 227–28, 255–56.

56. Alerding, *Diocese of Vincennes*, 351–52, 472–73; Alerding, *Diocese of Fort Wayne*, 277–78; Timothy E. Howard, *A History of St. Joseph County, Indiana* (Chicago: Lewis Publishing, 1907), 1:417–20; Aylward, "Immigrant Settlement Patterns in South Bend," 5–6; Young, *History of Wayne County*, 408; *History of Wayne County, Indiana*, 2:152–53.

57. Rebecca A. Shepherd et al., *A Biographical Directory of the Indiana General Assembly, 1816–1899* (Indianapolis: Indiana Historical Bureau, 1980), 1:104–05.

58. Thornbrough, *Indiana in the Civil War*, 60; Barnhart and Carmony, *Indiana*, 1:398–99, 2:97; Poinsatte, *Fort Wayne during the Canal Era*, 46:228–29; Hinkle, "Irish Immigrants in Terre Haute," 86.

59. Thornbrough, *Indiana in the Civil War*, 60–61, 634, 639; Barnhart and Carmony, *Indiana*, 2:141; Richardt, "History of Saint Joseph Church," 39; Carl F. Brand, "History of the Know Nothing Party in Indiana," *Indiana Magazine of History*, 18 (March 1922): 53, 72–73; Ibid., (June 1922): 177.

60. *Terre Haute Daily Wabash Express* quoted in Richardt, "History of Saint Joseph Church," 39–40.

61. Brand, "Know Nothing Party," 68, 76, 202, 284, 297; Stormont, *History of Gibson County*, 97; Thornbrough, *Indiana in the Civil War*, 76–77, 640.

62. Shepherd et al., *Biographical Directory . . . 1816–1899*, 1:37, 296, 373; Justin E. Walsh, *The Centennial History of the Indiana General Assembly, 1816–1978* (Indianapolis: Indiana Historical Bureau, 1987), 115, 721.

63. Richardt, "History of Saint Joseph Church," 32; Poinsatte, *Fort Wayne during the Canal Era*, 46:228; Jefferson Co.-261.4-Irish, microfilm, roll 11, frame 1165, Bartholomew Co.-261.4-Irish, microfilm, roll 1, frame 1865, IFWPP.

CHAPTER 3. NATIVES OF IRELAND AND URBAN COMMUNITY BUILDING: 1860–1920

1. See Table A, p. 38; Clifton J. Phillips, *Indiana in Transition: The Emergence of an Industrial Commonwealth, 1880–1920* (Indianapolis: Indiana Historical Bureau and Indiana Historical Society, 1968), 369.

2. See Table B, p. 41; U. S. Bureau of the Census, *Fourteenth Census of the United States Taken in the Year 1920*, vol. 3, *Population 1920, Composition and Characteristics of the Population By States* (Washington, DC: Government Printing Office, 1922), 303–04.

3. See Table B, p. 41.

4. *History of the Ohio Falls Cities and Their Counties* (Cleveland: L. A. Williams and Co., 1882), 2:310; Emma Lou Thornbrough, *Indiana in the Civil War Era, 1850–1880* (Indianapolis: Indiana Historical Bureau and Indiana Historical Society, 1965), 552; Urban Irish computations by author based on figures in *Population 1920*, 304, and U. S. Bureau of the Census, *A Report of the Seventeenth Decennial Census of the United States, Census of Population: 1950*, vol. 1, *Number of Inhabitants* (Washington, DC: Government Printing Office, 1952), 19.

5. Dean R. Esslinger, *Immigrants and the City: Ethnicity and Mobility in a Nineteenth-Century Midwestern Community* (Port Washington, NY: Kennikat Press, 1975), 88–89, 94–95; Jefferson Co.-261.4-Irish, microfilm, roll 11,

frame 1159, Indiana Federal Writers' Project/Program collection, Indiana State University Library, Terre Haute, Indiana (hereafter cited as IFWPP); Kathleen Van Nuys, *Indy International* (Indianapolis: Indianapolis News, 1978), 55; John Aylward, "Immigrant Settlement Patterns in South Bend, 1865–1917" (typescript, Northern Indiana Historical Society, 1971), 6.

6. Esslinger, *Immigrants and the City*, 52–54; Aylward, "Immigrant Settlement Patterns in South Bend," 5; "The Irish in Fort Wayne in 1880," Allen Co.-261.4-Irish, microfilm, roll 1, frame 0775, Jefferson Co.-261.4-Irish, microfilm, roll 11, frame 1160, Floyd Co.-261.4-Irish, microfilm, roll 7, frame 0558, Marion Co.-260.5-Ethnology, microfilm, roll 16, frame 0798, IFWPP; Frederick D. Kershner Jr., "From Country Town to Industrial City: The Urban Pattern in Indianapolis," *Indiana Magazine of History* 45 (December 1949): 329.

7. Thornbrough, *Indiana in the Civil War*, 126; William H. H. Terrell, *Indiana in the War of the Rebellion: Report of the Adjutant General* (1869, repr., Indianapolis: Indiana Historical Bureau, 1960), 1:561, 571; William H. H. Terrell, *Report of the Adjutant General of the State of Indiana* (Indianapolis: A. H. Conner, 1865–69), 2:352; B. R. Sulgrove, *History of Indianapolis and Marion County, Indiana* (Philadelphia: L. H. Everts and Co., 1884), 346; *History of Allen County, Indiana* (Chicago: Kingman Brothers, 1880), 72; Carl Wittke, *The Irish in America* (Baton Rouge: Louisiana State University Press, 1956), 142.

8. William R. Holloway, *Indianapolis: A Historical and Statistical Sketch of the Railroad City* (Indianapolis: Indianapolis Journal Print, 1870), 179–80.

9. Thornbrough, *Indiana in the Civil War*, 552–53; Phillips, *Indiana in Transition*, 465; Holloway, *Indianapolis*, 179–80, 257; *Indianapolis City Directory, 1878*, 68; *Indianapolis City Directory, 1883*, 39; Sulgrove, *History of Indianapolis*, 407; *Terre Haute City Directory and Business Mirror for 1858*, 28; *Terre Haute City Directory, 1915–16*, 76; *Biographical Record and Portrait Album of Tippecanoe County, Indiana* (Chicago: Lewis Publishing, 1888), 301; *Fort Wayne City Directory, 1874–75*, 290; Charles E. Robert, *Evansville: Her Commerce and Manufactures* (Evansville: Courier, 1874), 514; *Evansville City Directory, 1892*, 54; Thomas B. Helm, ed., *History of Cass County, Indiana* (Chicago: Brant and Fuller, 1886), 451.

10. Wittke, *Irish in America*, 196–97; Kerby A. Miller, *Emigrants and Exiles: Ireland and the Irish Exodus to North America* (New York: Oxford University Press, 1985), 533–34; Philip Flanagan, "The Ancient Order of Hibernians," Marion Co.-261.4-Irish, microfilm, roll 16, frame 0818, IFWPP; *Terre Haute City Directory, 1879–80*, 267; *Album of Tippecanoe County*, 301; Helm, *History of Cass County*, 452, 537; Timothy E. Howard, *A History of St. Joseph County, Indiana* (Chicago: Lewis Publishing, 1907), 1:462.

11. *Indianapolis City Directory, 1874*, 503; *Indianapolis City Directory, 1878*, 74; *Indianapolis City Directory, 1879*, 55, 63; *Indianapolis City Directory, 1882*, 52; *Indianapolis City Directory, 1886*, 69; *Indianapolis City Directory, 1889*, 93; *Indianapolis City Directory, 1900*, 134; *Indianapolis City Directory, 1898*, 134.

12. *Indianapolis City Directory, 1876*, 619; *Evansville City Directory, 1885*, 31; *Terre Haute City Directory, 1904*, 62; *Terre Haute City Directory, 1920*, 44; Herman J. Alerding, *The Diocese of Fort Wayne, 1857–September 22, 1907: A Book of Historical Reference, 1669–1907* (Fort Wayne, IN: Archer Printing, 1907), 204.

13. *Indianapolis City Directory, 1881*, 60; *Terre Haute City Directory, 1882*, 64; Holloway, *Indianapolis*, 292, 294; *Indianapolis City Directory, 1890*, 79, 81; *Indianapolis City Directory, 1898*, 122; *Indianapolis City Directory, 1878*, 68; *Terre Haute City Directory, 1879–80*, 268; *Terre Haute City Directory, 1900*, 37.

14. Thornbrough, *Indiana in the Civil War*, 552–53; Phillips, *Indiana in Transition*, 465; *Indianapolis City Directory, 1879*, 56; *Terre Haute City Directory, 1879–80*, 268; Jehu Z. Powell, ed., *History of Cass County, Indiana* (Chicago: Lewis Publishing, 1913), 1:224–25; Van Nuys, *Indy International*, 57.

15. Thornbrough, *Indiana in the Civil War*, 553; Allen Co.-261.4-Irish, microfilm, roll 1, frame 0775, IFWPP.

16. Allen Co.-261.4-Irish, microfilm, roll 1, frame 0775, IFWPP; Van Nuys, *Indy International*, 55.

17. Herman J. Alerding, *A History of the Catholic Church in the Diocese of Vincennes* (Indianapolis: Carlon and Hollenbeck, 1883), 335–37, 431, 458; Alerding, *Diocese of Fort Wayne*, 320–21, 277–78, 351–52, 395–96; *Ohio Falls Cities*, 2:446–47; J. Lawrence Richardt, "A Narrative History of Saint Joseph Church, Terre Haute, Indiana, 1838–1872" (master's thesis, Indiana State

University, 1969), 60; Helm, *History of Cass County*, 437; Powell, *History of Cass County*, 1:436; Howard, *History of St. Joseph County*, 1:421–22; Esslinger, *Immigrants and the City*, 28, 112–13; Aylward, "Immigrant Settlement Patterns in South Bend," 7; Holloway, *Indianapolis*, 182, 240–41; Sulgrove, *History of Indianapolis*, 407; Archibald Shaw, ed., *History of Dearborn County, Indiana, Her People, Industries and Institutions* (Indianapolis: B. F. Bowen and Co., 1915), 404; Robert, *Evansville: Her Commerce and Manufactures*, 534; Joseph P. Elliott, *A History of Evansville and Vanderburgh County, Indiana* (Evansville: Keller Printing, 1897), 279.

    18. Rebecca A. Shepherd et al., eds., *A Biographical Directory of the Indiana General Assembly, 1816–1899* (Indianapolis: Indiana Historical Bureau, 1980), 1:256; Justin E. Walsh, ed., *A Biographical Directory of the Indiana General Assembly, 1900–1984* (Indianapolis: Indiana Historical Bureau, 1984), 2:222, 407; Phillips, *Indiana in Transition*, 588.

    19. Urban Irish computations by author based on figures in U. S. Bureau of the Census, *Fourteenth Census of the United States Taken in the Year 1920*, vol. 3, *Population 1920, Composition and Characteristics of the Population By States* (Washington, DC: Government Printing Office, 1922), 307, 308; Aylward, "Immigrant Settlement Patterns in South Bend," 7; Van Nuys, *Indy International*, 57.

    20. See Table A, p. 38, and Table B, p. 41; U. S. Bureau of the Census, *Thirteenth Census of the United States Taken in the Year 1910*, vol. 2, *Population 1910, Reports By States, with Statistics for Counties, Cities and Other Civil Divisions, Alabama–Montana* (Washington, DC: Government Printing Office, 1913), 548; Philip R. VanderMeer, *The Hoosier Politician: Officeholding and Political Culture in Indiana, 1896–1920* (Urbana: University of Illinois Press, 1985), 124.

    21. Alerding, *Diocese of Fort Wayne*, 204; Powell, *History of Cass County*, 1:398; *Terre Haute City Directory, 1920*, 44.

    22. Hasia R. Diner, *Erin's Daughters in America: Irish Immigrant Women in the Nineteenth Century* (Baltimore: Johns Hopkins University Press, 1983), 107–08; John J. D. Trenor, "Proposals Affecting Immigration," *The Annals of the American Academy of Political and Social Science* 24 (July–December 1904): 229.

    23. Shepherd et al., *Biographical Directory . . . 1816–1899*, 1:130, 248; Van Nuys, *Indy International*, 56–57; Shaw, *History of Dearborn County*, 911; R. P. DeHart, ed., *Past and Present of Tippecanoe County, Indiana*

(Indianapolis: B. F. Bowen and Co., 1909), 2:862; Walsh, *Biographical Directory . . . 1900–1984*, 2:407; *Pictorial and Biographical Memoirs of Indianapolis and Marion County, Indiana* (Chicago: Goodspeed Brothers, 1893), 150.

    24. Phillips, *Indiana in Transition*, 464; Charles Blanchard, ed., *History of the Catholic Church in Indiana* (Logansport, IN: A. W. Bowen and Co., 1898), 1:94, 105; Sulgrove, *History of Indianapolis*, 407; Alerding, *Diocese of Vincennes*, 432, 434; *Terre Haute City Directory, 1894*, 30; *Terre Haute City Directory, 1900*, 19.

    25. VanderMeer, *Hoosier Politician*, 48; Wittke, *Irish in America*, 113; *Memoirs of Indianapolis and Marion County*, 128–29; Shaw, *History of Dearborn County*, 1007–09; Walsh, *Biographical Directory . . . 1900–1984*, 2:321.

    26. Edward A. Leary, *Indianapolis: The Story of a City* (Indianapolis: Bobbs-Merrill, 1971), 122–23, 146–47.

    27. Shepherd et al., *Biographical Directory . . . 1816–1899*, 1:97, 123, 176, 192–93, 231, 248, 253, 297, 380–81; DeHart, *Past and Present of Tippecanoe County*, 2:862; Shaw, *History of Dearborn County*, 556–57, 910–11; *Biographical and Historical Souvenir for the Counties of Clark, Crawford, Harrison, Floyd, Jefferson, Jennings, Scott, and Washington, Indiana* (Chicago: John M. Gresham and Co., 1889), 2:100–01.

    28. Helm, *History of Cass County*, 536–37; Shepherd et al., *Biographical Directory . . . 1816–1899*, 1:163, 380–81; Walsh, *Biographical Directory . . . 1900–1984*, 2:222.

    29. Shepherd et al., *Biographical Directory . . . 1816–1899*, 1:37, 192–93, 328, 351.

    30. Justin E. Walsh, *The Centennial History of the Indiana General Assembly, 1816–1978* (Indianapolis: Indiana Historical Bureau, 1987), 258–59, 399, 703, 721; VanderMeer, *Hoosier Politician*, 126–33, 140–42.

    31. Wittke, *Irish in America*, 153–57, 197–98; Thornbrough, *Indiana in the Civil War*, 553; Holloway, *Indianapolis*, 280.

    32. Wittke, *Irish in America*, 164–66; Miller, *Emigrants and Exiles*, 539–40; *The New York Times*, May 19, 20, 1880; *Indianapolis City Directory, 1881*, 60; *Indianapolis City Directory, 1883*, 39; *Indianapolis City Directory, 1885*, 41; *Indianapolis City Directory, 1886*, 60.

    33. Phillips, *Indiana in Transition*, 588–89; John D. Barnhart and Donald F. Carmony, *Indiana: From Frontier to Industrial Commonwealth* (New York: Lewis Publishing, 1954), 2:375–76.

CHAPTER 4. DESCENDANTS OF IMMIGRANTS AND IRISH IDENTITY:
1920–2000

1. Table A, p. 38; Table B, p. 41.

2. Clifton J. Phillips, *Indiana in Transition: The Emergence of an Industrial Commonwealth, 1880–1920* (Indianapolis: Indiana Historical Bureau and Indiana Historical Society, 1968), 368–69; Table A, p. 38; Kathleen Van Nuys, *Indy International* (Indianapolis: Indianapolis News, 1978), 57; Dennis Clark, *Hibernia America: The Irish and Regional Cultures* (New York: Greenwood Press, 1986), 131.

3. Herman J. Alerding, *A History of the Catholic Church in the Diocese of Vincennes* (Indianapolis: Carlon and Hollenbeck, 1883), 453, 459; Floyd Co.-261.4-Irish, microfilm, roll 7, frame 0558, roll 1, frame 0775, Allen Co.-261.4-Irish, microfilm, roll 1, frame 0775, Jefferson Co.-261.4-Irish, microfilm, roll 11, frame 1160, Indiana Federal Writers' Project/Program collection, Indiana State University Library, Terre Haute, Indiana (hereafter cited as IFWPP); *Terre Haute City Directory, 1904,* 62; *Terre Haute City Directory, 1927,* 26; Marion Co.-261.4-Irish, microfilm, roll 16, frame 0818, IFWPP.

4. Robert S. Lynd and Helen Merrell Lynd, *Middletown: A Study in Contemporary American Culture* (New York: Harcourt, Brace and Co., 1929), 293, 332; Clark, *Hibernia America,* 124; Dubois Co.-260.5-Ethnology, microfilm, roll 5, frame 1882, IFWPP.

5. Marion Co.-260.5-Ethnology, microfilm, roll 16, frame 0798, IFWPP.

6. Ernie Hernandez, *Ethnics in Northwest Indiana* (Gary: Post-Tribune, 1984), 154; Table B, p. 41; Table C, p. 76; Floyd Co.-260.5-Ethnology, microfilm, roll 7, frame 0561, Marion Co.-261.4-Irish, microfilm, roll 16, frames 0818–0819, Bartholomew Co.-261.4-Irish, microfilm, roll 1, frame 1865, IFWPP; Justin E. Walsh, ed., *A Biographical Directory of the Indiana General Assembly, 1900–1984* (Indianapolis: Indiana Historical Bureau, 1984), 2:76.

7. Leonard Dinnerstein and David M. Reimers, *Ethnic Americans: A History of Immigration and Assimilation,* 2nd ed. (New York: Harper and Row Publishers, 1982), 110; Van Nuys, *Indy International,* 56.

8. Frederick D. Kershner Jr., "From Country Town to Industrial City: The Urban Pattern in Indianapolis," *Indiana Magazine of History* 45

(December 1949): 329; Van Nuys, *Indy International*, 55, 56, 57; John H. Fenton, *Midwest Politics* (New York: Holt, Rinehart and Winston, 1966), 175; Walsh, *Biographical Directory . . . 1900–1984*, 2:277.

9. Justin E. Walsh, *The Centennial History of the Indiana General Assembly, 1816–1978* (Indianapolis: Indiana Historical Bureau, 1987), 566, 703, 721; Walsh, *Biographical Directory . . . 1900–1984*, 2:145, 238, 257, 279–80, 320, 364; "Governor Remains in Critical Condition," *Indianapolis Star*, September 13, 2003.

10. Table A, p. 38; The exact number of persons reporting Irish ancestry was 965,602, U. S. Bureau of the Census, "Selected Social Characteristics: 1990, Indiana" [1990 CPH-L-80. Table1] (Ethnic History Project, Indiana Historical Society); Hernandez, *Ethnics in Northwest Indiana*, 153.

11. Van Nuys, *Indy International*, 56.

12. *The Criterion*, January 17, 1992; *Indianapolis Star*, January 11, 16, 17, 1992.

13. Hernandez, *Ethnics in Northwest Indiana*, 154; Michael F. Funchion, ed., *Irish American Voluntary Organizations* (Westport, CT: Greenwood Press, 1983), 61; Nationalities Council of Indiana, Club List (Ethnic History Project, Indiana Historical Society, 1992); "Metro Briefs," *South Bend Tribune*, December 9, 2004; Jack McGinley of Indianapolis, telephone interview with author, October 22, 1992; "Welcome," Kevin Barry Division of the Ancient Order of Hibernians, http://www.geocities.com/Area51/Corridor/2148/irish.html (accessed October 26, 2005); Benjamin Cashman of South Bend, telephone interview with author, February 21, 2005.

14. Dinnerstein and Reimers, *Ethnic Americans*, 190–99; John Hope Franklin and Alfred A. Moss Jr., *From Slavery to Freedom: A History of African Americans* (Boston: McGraw-Hill, 2000), 580–81; "Who We Are," Indiana Irish Cultural Society (Indianapolis, n.d.), http://www.indyirish.org/ (accessed October 26, 2005); "Welcome to the Keough Institute for Irish Studies" (Notre Dame, IN: University of Notre Dame, 2005), http://www.nd.edu/~irishstu/ (accessed October 26, 2005).

15. Franklin and Moss, *From Slavery to Freedom*, 580–81; "*Roots*: U.S. Serial Drama," in *The Encyclopedia of Television*, Horace Newcomb, ed. (Chicago: Museum of Broadcast Communications, 2004), http://www.

museum.tv/archives/etv, (accessed October 26, 2005); Valerie Gladstone, "The Man Behind the Duel between Irish Blockbusters," *New York Times*, March 2, 1997.

16. Robert M. Taylor Jr. and Connie A. McBirney, eds., *Peopling Indiana: The Ethnic Experience* (Indianapolis: Indiana Historical Society, 1996).

17. Sheila K. Ter Meer, "A Bit of the Irish," *Terre Haute Tribune-Star*, March 16, 1992; Patrick H. Cahill of Terre Haute, telephone interview with author, October 22, 1992; Jim Bolin of Terre Haute, telephone interview with author, October 22, 1992; Sandy Boyles-Gillen of Terre Haute, interview with author, February 23, 2005; Sharon B. Hinkle, "Irish Immigrants in Terre Haute, Indiana, in 1860: A Comparative Study" (master's thesis, Indiana State University, 1987); Trevor Gordon, "Indiana's Voice: The Irish National Land League in the Hoosier State: 1879–1882" (master's thesis, Indiana State University, 2001).

18. Pat Spellacy of Indianapolis, telephone interview with author, October 21, 1992; Juanita Taylor of Indianapolis, telephone interview with author, October 21, 1992; Nationalities Council of Indiana Web site (Indianapolis: Indiana University-Purdue University at Indianapolis, 2005), http://www.nationalitiescouncil.org/nci.html (accessed October 26, 2005).

19. Alice Field Davis of Indianapolis, telephone interview with author, February 11, 2005; "State, Division, and Links," Ladies Ancient Order of Hibernians, Our Lady of Knock Division, Indianapolis, Indiana Web page, (Indianapolis: Indy's Irish Festival, 2005), http://www.indyirishfest.com/links/laoh.html (accessed October 26, 2005).

20. Davis, interview with author; "Emerald Society, Pipe Band History," Indianapolis Firefighters Emerald Society Pipes and Drums Web site (Indianapolis: IQuest, n.d.), http://indypipes.org/History.html (accessed October 26, 2005); "History," Indiana Emerald Society (N.p., WebRing, n. d.), http://home.insightbb.com/~indianaemerald/ (accessed October 26, 2005).

21. "Who We Are," Indiana Irish Cultural Society.

22. Davis, interview with author; Indy's Irish Festival Web site (Indianapolis: Indy's Irish Festival, 2005), http://indyirishfest.com (accessed October 26, 2005); "The Indiana Irish Cultural Society Welcomes You to the Indianapolis Feis" ([Indianapolis: Indiana Irish Cultural Society], n.d.), http://indyfeis.org/ (accessed October 26, 2005).

23. Taylor, interview with author; Davis, interview with author.

24. Becky Tull, "Shamrock Club for Irish Only," *South Bend Tribune*, January 31, 1994; Andrew S. Hughes, "Makem Band Gets St. Pat's Festivities Off to Early Start," *South Bend Tribune*, March 3, 1994; "Celebrations on Tap for St. Patrick's Day," *South Bend Tribune*, March 13, 1994; Becky Emmons, "Carpet Out for First St. Patrick's Parade," *South Bend Tribune*, March 13, 1997; Jason Kelly, "It's a Parade," *South Bend Tribune*, March 12, 1998; "Hundreds Fight Chill for Irish Parade," *South Bend Tribune*, March 15, 1998; Don Porter, "Irish Eyes Smiling with 1,000 at Event," *South Bend Tribune*, March 17, 1999.

25. Alan S. Bigger, e-mail to author, February 7, 2005; "About Us," South Bend Shamrock Club Web site (South Bend, IN: South Bend Shamrock Club, n.d.), http://www.sbshamrockclub.com/index.html (accessed October 26, 2005).

26. "Press Release Band Bio," "Celtic Fire," Kennedy's Kitchen Web site (N.p.: Kennedy's Kitchen, [2005]), http://kennedyskitchen.com/ (accessed October 27, 2005); "About Our House," Fiddler's Hearth Public House Web site (South Bend, IN: Fiddler's Hearth, 2003), http://fiddlers hearth.com/index.html (accessed October 27, 2005); *Celtic Traditions* program listed in "Departments: Specialty Departments," on 88.9 WSND-FM Web site (Notre Dame, IN: WSND-FM, 2004), http://www.nd.edu/~wsnd/index.html (accessed October 27, 2005); Mike Stack, "Cagan's Irish Stop Keeps Wearin' o' the Green Year Round," *South Bend Tribune*, May 5, 1997.

27. Boyles-Gillen, interview with author.

CONCLUSION

1. David Ward, *Poverty, Ethnicity, and the American City, 1840–1925: Changing Conceptions of the Slum and the Ghetto* (New York: Cambridge University Press, 1989).

2. Kevin Kenny, ed., *New Directions in Irish American History* (Madison: University of Wisconsin Press, 2003).

Selected Bibliography

Bhroimeil, Una Ni. *Building Irish Identity in America, 1870–1915: The Gaelic Revival.* Dublin: Four Courts, 2003.

Blessing, Patrick J. *The Irish in America: A Guide to the Literature and the Manuscript Collections.* Washington, DC: Catholic University of America Press, 1992.

Callahan, Nelson J., and William F. Hinkey. *Irish Americans and Their Communities in Cleveland.* Cleveland: Cleveland State University, 1978.

Dezell, Maureen. *Irish America: Coming into Clover: The Evolution of a People and a Culture.* New York: Doubleday, 2001.

Diner, Hasia R. *Erin's Daughters in America: Irish Immigrant Women in the Nineteenth Century.* Baltimore: Johns Hopkins University Press, 1983.

Elliott, Bruce S. *Irish Emigrants in Canada: A New Approach.* 2nd ed. Montreal: McGill-Queen's University Press, 2004.

Emmons, David M. *The Butte Irish: Class and Ethnicity in an American Mining Town, 1875–1925.* Urbana: University of Illinois Press, 1989.

Fanning, Charles, ed. *New Perspectives on the Irish Diaspora.* Carbondale: Southern Illinois University Press, 2000.

Flannery, John B. *The Irish Texans.* San Antonio: University of Texas, Institute of Texan Cultures at San Antonio, 1980.

Gallman, J. Matthew. *Receiving Erin's Children: Philadelphia, Liverpool, and the Irish Famine Migration, 1845–1855.* Chapel Hill: University of North Carolina Press, 2000.

Glazier, Michael, ed. *Encyclopedia of the Irish in America.* Notre Dame: University of Notre Dame Press, 1999.

Gleeson, David T. *The Irish in the South, 1815–1877.* Chapel Hill: University of North Carolina Press, 2001.

Greeley, Andrew M. *The Irish Americans: The Rise to Money and Power.* New York: Harper and Row, 1981.

Griffin, Patrick. *The People with No Name: Ireland's Ulster Scots, America's Scots Irish, and the Creation of a British Atlantic World, 1689–1764.* Princeton: Princeton University Press, 2001.

Handlin, Oscar. *Boston's Immigrants, 1790–1880: A Study in Accultura-tion.* Cambridge: Belknap Press of Harvard University Press, 1959.

Herr, Cheryl T. *Critical Regionalism and Cultural Studies: From Ireland to the American Midwest.* Gainesville: University Press of Florida, 1996.

Holmes, David G. *Irish in Wisconsin.* Madison: Wisconsin Historical Society Press, 2004.

Holmquist, June Drenning, ed. *They Chose Minnesota: A Survey of the State's Ethnic Groups.* St. Paul: Minnesota Historical Society Press, 1981.

Kenny, Kevin. *Making Sense of the Molly Maguires.* New York: Oxford University Press, 1998.

——. *The American Irish: A History.* New York: Longman, 2000.

——, ed. *New Directions in Irish American History.* Madison: University of Wisconsin Press, 2003.

Lang, Elfrieda. "Irishmen in Northern Indiana before 1850." *Mid-America: An Historical Review* 36 (1954): 190–98.

McCaffrey, Lawrence J. *The Irish Catholic Diaspora in America.* Wash-ington, DC: Catholic University of America Press, 1997.

Meagner, Timothy J. *Inventing Irish America: Generation, Class, and Ethnic Identity in a New England City, 1880–1928.* Notre Dame: University of Notre Dame Press, 2001.

Miller, Kerby A. *Emigrants and Exiles: Ireland and the Irish Exodus to North America.* New York: Oxford University Press, 1985.

Moran, Gerard. *Sending Out Ireland's Poor: Assisted Emigration to North America in the Nineteenth Century.* Dublin: Four Courts, 2004.

Niehaus, Earl F. *The Irish in New Orleans, 1860–1900.* Baton Rouge: Louisiana State University Press, 1965.

O'Connor, Thomas H. *The Boston Irish: A Political History.* Boston: Northeastern University, 1995.

Taylor, Robert M., Jr., and Connie A. McBirney, eds. *Peopling Indiana: The Ethnic Experience.* Indianapolis: Indiana Historical Society, 1996.

Quinlan, Kieran. *Strange Kin: Ireland and the American South.* Baton Rouge: Louisiana State University Press, 2005.

Quinn, Dermot. *The Irish in New Jersey: Four Centuries of American Life.* New Brunswick: Rutgers University Press, 2004.

Quinn, John F. *Father Mathew's Crusade: Temperance in Nineteenth-Century Ireland and Irish America.* Amherst: University of Massachusetts Press, 2002.

Regan, Ann. *Irish in Minnesota.* St. Paul: Minnesota Historical Society Press, 2002.

Wilson, David A. *United Irishmen, United States: Immigrant Radicals in the Early Republic.* Ithaca: Cornell University Press, 1998.

Wittke, Carl F. *The Irish in America.* Baton Rouge: Louisiana State University Press, 1956.

Index

Page numbers in boldface indicate illustrations and tables.

Flanigan, Patrick, 80–81
Flannagan family, 34
Floyd County, 39, 40, 41, 42; Catholic
 Settlement, 15, 34, 53, 80; Foreign
 Settlement, 15; St. Mary, 34, 80
Flynn, William P., 81
Foley, Daniel, 66
Ford, John, 50
Foreign Settlement (Floyd County), 15
Fort Miamis, 6
Fort Ouiatenon, 6, 8
Fort Wayne: beginnings of Wabash
 and Erie Canal, 17; burial markers
 along canal, 22; Catholic families,
 14; changing Irish residential
 patterns, 78; early days of the canal,
 21; Hibernians, 66; increase of
 Catholic population, 30–31; Irish
 Catholic Benevolent Association,
 58; "Irish Town," 55; number of
 canal construction workers, 20; St.
 Augustine, 31
Francois, Rev. John Claude, 31
French, 6, 9, 14
French and Indian War, 8
French Jesuit priests, 14
Friendly Sons of Erin (Lake County),
 84
Friendly Sons of St. Patrick
 (Indianapolis), 60–61
Fruits, Katherine Margaret O'Connell,
 82–83
Fur trade, 6–7; license, **6**

Gary, 65; St. Luke, 79
Gavazzi, Rev. Alessandro, 48
Germans: Catholic population in Fort
 Wayne, 30; parishes, 47; workers
 on National Road construction, 27;
 workers on Wabash and Erie Canal,
 18, 21

Gibson County, 49; cholera, 36;
 construction of Wabash and Erie
 Canal, 36
Golden Ace Inn (Indianapolis), 92
Gordon, Trevor, 88
Gorman, Michael, 63
G. P. McGoughall and Son
 (Indianapolis), 66
Graham, William, 12
Grant County, 41, 52, 53
Griffin's County Kerry Pub
 (Indianapolis), 92
Gurley, Boyd, 77

Haggerty, James, 72
Half Way to St. Pat's Day parties, 93
Hall, Noreen, 84
Hamilton County, 76
Haney, N., 60
Hanlon, Thomas, 71
Hannagan, Stephen J., 67, 71
Harrison, William Henry, 6, 11
Hefron, David J., 70
Hendricks County, 76
Hibernian Benevolent Society, 58,
 65–66
Hibernian Rifles (Indianapolis), 61
Hinkle, Sharon Bryant, 88
Holy Cross (Indianapolis), 33
Holy Trinity Parish (New Albany), 34
Howard, Timothy E., **70**, 71
Howard County, 76
Huntington, 20

Indiana Constitutional Convention
 (1816), 12
Indiana Emerald Society (Evansville),
 90
Indiana Federal Writers' Project/
 Program (IFWPP), 55–56, 78–79,
 96